L · E · A · R · N

Playful Techniques
to Accelerate Learning

L · E · A · R · N

Playful Techniques
to Accelerate Learning

Regina G. Richards

Zephyr
Press

TUCSON, ARIZONA

LEARN
Playful Techniques to Accelerate Learning

Grades K–12

© 1993 by Zephyr Press

Printed in the United States of America

ISBN 0-913705-89-6

Editors: Stacey Lynn and Stacey Shropshire
Cover design: Nancy Taylor
Design and production: Nancy Taylor
Back cover photo courtesy Madison Photography

Zephyr Press
P.O. Box 66006
Tucson, Arizona 85728-6006

Richards, Regina G.
    Learn : playful techniques to accelerate learning / Regina G.
  Richards.
        p.   cm.
    Includes bibliographical references.
    ISBN 0-913705-89-6
    1. Learning, Psychology of. 2. Mnemonics. 3. Visual learning.
  I. Title.
  LB1060.R53 1993
  370. 15'23—dc20   93-21956

Printed on recycled paper.

The secret of education lies in respecting the pupil.

—Ralph Waldo Emerson

Contents

Foreword

In the midst of the transformation now sweeping through American education, teachers must continue to gather their students about them daily and facilitate learning. While school boards conduct surveys to meet the community's demands for greater accountability, superintendents forge guidelines for restructuring relationships between the schools and local businesses, curriculum developers apply cross-disciplinary approaches to reconfiguring programs, and school-based committees study the criteria for evaluating the merits of authentic assessments, it is up to us teachers to establish tranquility in our classrooms and see to it that our pupils learn.

Learning is a natural process. The brain does it automatically. Whether through deliberate imitation or random exploration, our minds are constantly exposed to new facts and new feats. When fresh information brings us pleasure, our memory prods us to seek opportunities to repeat the experience. If we recall an event as a source of pain, we avoid duplicating it in the future. Our experiences are remembered. We learn from them.

Teachers do not *cause* learning. They can, however, enhance the students' chances for successful growth and development. By consciously controlling the classroom environment, teachers can reduce the risk of failure so that *all* students feel that it is safe to try, it is possible to succeed, and it is worth the effort.

Within the confines of our classrooms—regardless of the fact that we are often forced to teach within limitations imposed on us by insufficient funds, inadequate materials, ill-prepared students, unenlightened supervisors, and uninspiring administrators—it is possible for us to establish a learning environment where even the most unmotivated students can taste the joys of academic achievement. Those who find it difficult to achieve academically will not attempt learning until someone acts to motivate them by building interest and stimulating courage. Those who are already successful in school will always welcome any technique that makes learning easier and more efficient.

If we create an atmosphere where every class member finds

- it is safe to try
- it is possible to succeed
- it is worth the effort

then every student becomes interested, cooperative, and motivated.

Successful students don't cause trouble. Successful students don't drop out. Successful students learn as fast as they can and as slowly as they have to. They understand the way the mind works and have a whole arsenal of techniques to facilitate their own learning. Successful students are confident of their own ability to develop skills and acquire knowledge. Successful students have taken the first step toward becoming lifelong learners.

All the learning strategies introduced in Regina Richards's book *LEARN: Playful Techniques to Accelerate Learning* have the potential for transforming a student's chances for successful academic performance into realized goals. The reason the strategies are useful can be explained by modern brain research. Their effectiveness has been demonstrated through carefully controlled scientific studies. We now know that the methods outlined in this book are appropriate and practical tools for enhancing the learning of all students. They offer an ideal means for teachers to stimulate interest, enhance concentration, increase understanding, and improve memory. Those who take the time to master these techniques almost always get a startling improvement in student performance.

I salute all who have the courage to try.

Happy teaching.

Suzanne H. Stevens
Learning disability specialist, author
November 1992

Acknowledgments

Ideas, ideas, ideas . . . where have my ideas come from? My ideas have come from books I've read over the years, colleagues I've worked with, conference speakers, casual chats with other conference participants, and teachers who have taken classes I've taught—especially the more interactive ones who have offered ideas and suggestions. The list is endless. It's impossible to evaluate thoroughly the depth of influence individual persons have had on my thinking and the development of my teaching strategies and philosophies. Of particular influence has been the field of developmental optometry, with its tremendous emphasis on training people to use visualization. There are particular authors and researchers whose work has laid many of the foundations upon which my philosophies are based: optometrist Gerald Getman, author Suzanne Stevens, author Jane Healy, Scott Bornstein and Arthur Bornstein of the Bornstein School of Memory, and many more.

I've worked with countless students over the years, and I often think that these fine youngsters have had the greatest influence on my philosophies. Their frustrations, their courage, their stamina—these have all encouraged me to seek alternative ways to present ideas, concepts, and strategies. These students are the real basis for any inspirations that have occurred. The challenge to make a learning task easier always provides a great stimulus to develop a more creative, effective way to help students perform the task.

To all these people, I give my grateful thanks.

Special thanks are extended to two professionals and colleagues who have contributed to this work. I thank Suzanne Stevens, author and learning disability specialist, for the very fine and enthusiastic foreword. Dr. Beth Ballinger's expertise as a developmental optometrist has encouraged me over the years to think about the processes involved in developing visualization. I have greatly enjoyed our association and many stimulating discussions, and I thank Beth for her tremendous assistance in previewing chapter 2 and for adding her optometric perspective to that chapter.

I thank Marshall Welch of the University of Utah for his permission to use the PLEASE strategy (chapter 6). The following publishers were very gracious in granting permission to include their materials in various chapters of *LEARN:* Academic Therapy Publications gave permission to use MFR pictures in chapter 6 and Getman's data from VSA in chapter 2; Aspen Systems Corporation gave permission to use portions from Pehrsson and Robinson's *Semantic Organizer Approach* and Pehrsson and Denner's *Semantic Organizers* in chapter 8; Bantam Doubleday Dell Publishing Group allowed me to use Healy's mind map of the Civil War from *Your Child's Growing Mind* in chapter 8; Educator's Publishing Service allowed me to use Gillingham's Stream of Language illustration from her *Remedial Training* in chapter 5; and the Optometric Extension Program Foundation gave permission to use Hendrickson's four steps to enhance visual memory in chapter 2. The Peanuts cartoon in chapter 1 is reprinted by permission of UFS, Inc. (United Media).

Particular and extensive thanks go to the fine professionals in my office, with whom I've spent many hours brainstorming and discussing ideas, strategies, and methods that are successful with students who previously have not met with success using more traditional methods. In particular, Judy Love, educational therapist, who created the poems for the MFM system (Appendix B) and the cloud concept for prepositions (chapter 10), deserves a special acknowledgment. And thanks to Dindy S. Wheelock, speech and language therapist; Judith Fuhrman, speech and language therapist; Simone Acosta, educational therapist; Pam Meeker, educational therapist; Janine Monahan, educational therapist. Special thanks for contributions to the artwork go to Matthew Acosta (COPS dinosaur), Simone Acosta (MFM pictures), Becky Bane (COPS policeman and flower in chapter 1), Judith Fuhrman (MFM pictures), and Deedra Love-Dobis (visualization in chapter 2).

I thank Shannon Sears for helping me with the majority of the typing, as well as Lanny Rogers and Jennie Greenberg for their help. I thank Judy Love in my office for her continual assistance in proofreading. And I thank my editors at Zephyr Press, Stacey Lynn and Stacey Shropshire, for their help and guidance.

Special and loving thanks go to my husband, Irv, who has been so supportive and gracious about the many hours I've spent at his computer. My sons, Dov and Eli (since the real proof of any technique is in how well it translates into the home and homework environment), have my gratitude for their tolerance, patience, and willingness to use alternative strategies.

To all of you, and the many more whom I have not directly named, thank you!

1

The LEARN System, 4M and VIP

LEARN stands for **L**earning **E**fficiently **A**nd **R**emembering m**N**emonics. It is a system, a set of strategies, that helps students use a variety of processing styles to greater advantage. *Processing* refers to how we use information that comes to us through our senses. To understand processing, let's begin with a brief discussion of our wonderful brain, our instrument for processing.

The Incredible Brain

The human brain is amazing. Think of all that we accomplish under the direction of this organizer that weighs only three pounds. The brain governs basic body functions and behaviors, such as our ability to regulate body temperature, digest food, and stay alert or fall asleep. It is responsible for our most sophisticated activities and cradles our hopes, thoughts, emotions, and personality. The brain is complex, with many lobes, layers, and fissures. The number of neurons (nerve cells) in an average brain is thought to be a staggering one hundred billion. The number of possible interconnections between these cells is greater than the number of atoms in the universe.[1]

The cerebrum of the brain consists of two hemispheres, the right and the left. These hemispheres are connected by the corpus callosum, a bundle of commissural nerve fibers that serves as a facilitator for communication between the two hemispheres. This

Figure 1.1. Three Peanuts characters discuss their processing tendencies.

bundle is the largest fiber pathway in the brain. It covers about four inches and forms a bridge of about three hundred million nerve fibers, which become myelinated as we mature and gain experience. In the process of myelinization, the outer parts of neurons develop a waxy coating that "insulates the wiring and facilitates rapid and clear transmissions."[2]

Each hemisphere contains a motor strip as well as a sensory area, and these areas are symmetrical. The left side of the brain receives sensory information from and controls movement on the right side of the body. The right side of the brain receives information from and controls movement on the left side of the body. The brain is not totally symmetrical, however, and many specialized functions are centered primarily in one hemisphere or another. For example, the speech and hearing centers, called Broca's area, are generally on the left side of the brain, just above the ear. The left hemisphere tends to be more involved and more

proficient in language and logic, whereas the right hemisphere is more involved in controlling spatial activities and gestalt thinking. But it is an oversimplification to assume that the two hemispheres are separate systems, like two individual brains. Although each hemisphere is specialized to handle different tasks, the task division between the two hemispheres is not absolute, and they constantly communicate with each other. Neither hemisphere is completely idle while the other one is active. Most activities, especially one as complex as speaking, involve both hemispheres interacting with each other.

The cortex is the surface of the cerebrum and functions as a control panel for processing information at three levels: receiving sensory stimuli, organizing them into meaningful patterns so that we can make sense out of the world, and associating patterns to help develop abstract types of learning and thinking.[3]

Processing Styles

As human beings, we all use both hemispheres. No one is completely a right-hemisphere or a left-hemisphere person unless she or he has severe physiological damage. It has become popular, however, to refer to people by their processing tendency. We may say a person is a "right-hemisphere processor" or a "left-hemisphere processor" because, in many tasks, one or the other hemisphere takes control and acts in charge. Or we may say a person is right brain/left brain, global/linear, or a lumper/splitter.[4] Figure 1.1 humorously illustrates the extent to which such thinking permeates our culture. Clare Cherry has stated, "Given the asymmetrical physical difference of the hemispheres, it is not surprising that each deals with information in different ways."[5] These processing characteristics have been described quite extensively in the literature, including Cherry et al., Vitale, Stevens, and Healy.[6] Following are some of the processing characteristics typical of each hemisphere:

Left Hemisphere	Right Hemisphere
Linear—works with details rather than wholes	Holistic—works with wholes rather than parts
Concrete and precise	Metaphoric and symbolic
Sequential and systematic	Random and informal
Logical and uses planning	Intuitive and spontaneous
Verbal—processes language for meaning	Nonverbal—responds to body language
More auditory than visual	More visual than auditory
Reality based	Fantasy oriented
Automatic—recalls automatic codes	Responsive to novelty
Temporal—aware of time in past, present, future	Nontemporal—does not always consider time
Practical—concerned with cause and effect	Original—concerned with ideas and theories

These lists make it clear that the left hemisphere is more in control of symbolic and language activities and processes more details. The right hemisphere is used to process haptic (sense of touch), spatial, and global information.

Barbara Meister Vitale has identified many academic tasks that are related primarily to a specific processing style.[7] Following is how she describes the division of academic skills based on hemispheric specialization:

Left Hemisphere	Right Hemisphere
Handwriting	Haptic awareness
Symbols	Spatial relationships
Language	Shapes and patterns
Reading	Mathematical computation
Phonics	Color sensitivity
Locating details and facts	Singing and music
Talking and reciting	Art expression
Following directions	Creativity
Listening	Visualization

A *balance* usually exists between the hemispheres, with each taking control of the tasks it handles best and with the hemispheres working together as a coordinated unit. A task may have several components, and each hemisphere will handle the components that require the strength of that hemisphere. Some brains find certain processing modes more comfortable, so they tend to approach certain tasks with a preferred style—more global and holistic or more analytical. It is very similar to handedness. Most of us are more comfortable using our dominant hand and are more efficient using it in various tasks. However, we are quite capable of using both hands together, and in many situations we rely on the nondominant hand. Similarly, both hemispheres work in tandem and constantly integrate processing styles as the hemispheres deal with different aspects of a problem.

In general, the *left brain* codes and processes messages in language. It thinks by "talking to itself" as it manipulates numbers and words, and it plans using logic. It does not have a sense of space, but it is constantly aware of time and refers to an inner clock for much of its evaluation and organization.[8] The left brain breaks information into small, manageable pieces. It places these pieces into an order that helps organize and categorize material. It deals with this information in a very systematic manner, incorporating sequencing and step-by-step processing. In music, it attends to notations and lyrics. It helps language processing by ordering sounds and words, using function words, and mediating fine distinctions between words. The left brain stores factual information, and it reaches conclusions through *reasoning* and by being systematic, without feeling or emotions.

The *right brain* is primarily nonverbal and intuitive. It deals directly with reality through a mode of thinking that uses visual images and metaphors rather than words or numbers. It has a highly developed awareness of space, and much of its thinking involves imagining, imagery, or placing objects in space. The right brain takes in data as whole units and organizes information by seeking relationships and by recognizing similarities between wholes. It prefers analogous leaps to step-by-step processing. In music, it picks up the melody, and melodies frequently "float around" in the person's mind while he or she is engaged in other activities. The right brain helps process language through interpreting body language, prosody, and understanding the overall meaning. It produces sudden insights that serve as stepping stones to help it *feel* its way to conclusions by use of hunches or trial and error. It "knows intuitively by being sensitive, imaginative, and whimsical."[9] Figure 1.2 illustrates how people with different processing approaches would interpret the concept of a flower.

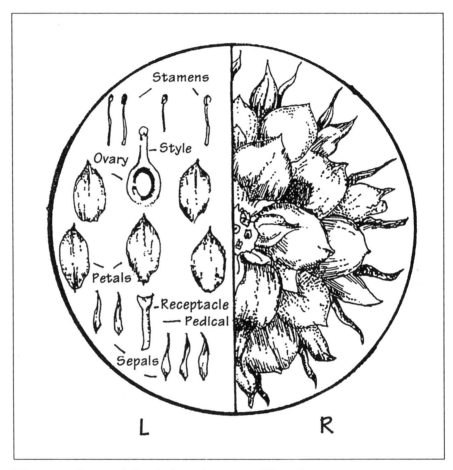

Figure 1.2. How each hemisphere interprets "flower"

Students who tend to rely on their right hemispheres often have very astute powers of observation and look at the world as if through a wide-angle lens. The "unspoken messages in the realm of feelings are noticed by these very perceptive children [who are] extremely adept at reading people."[10] These children use their observation skills to learn not only about people but also about objects and aspects of the environment. Following are descriptions of two students who have different processing styles.

Examples of Two Learning Styles

Eli

Eli is a fourteen-year-old student whose processing style exemplifies many characteristics of right-hemisphere functioning. He is a very bright and creative young man and has demonstrated this creativity since he was quite young. Even in second grade, he loved writing creative stories. Of course, his spelling was very creative also, but he enjoyed the process of imagining and expressing his ideas. As he got older, he wrote less and less. When someone asked him why, he would reply, "It's not fun any more. Now that I've learned all about that other garbage, like periods and capital letters and correct spelling, I have to think about too many things and it's no longer any fun to think of the story." His teachers and therapists have tried to persuade him to write his first draft without thinking of the mechanics, but they have not been successful. They hope that he will return to creative story writing.

Eli also doodles on his papers. Most of his assignments, whether for English or algebra, have faces in the margins, circles around the holes in the paper, or squiggles by his name. Sometimes, he states, he is not even aware he has been drawing.

It is very hard for Eli to sit still in class. Inevitably, he will be playing with a paper clip or taking apart a pen. Many teachers assume he is not listening, when in fact he is listening very intently. He just needs to be moving constantly.

Eli reports that he always hears music in his head. He says, "It's just there!" When he was younger the music would sometimes "escape" and all of a sudden, in the middle of class, he would start humming or singing. He has since learned that he cannot begin singing in the middle of a quiet classroom, especially during tests. He is now able to control this tendency fairly well. He says, however, that sometimes when he is memorizing vocabulary words or studying spelling, the music begins to interfere. He tries to take what he is memorizing and set it to the music, and doing so helps him remember the words.

Eli has extremely good spatial awareness and has demonstrated spatial skills since he was a toddler. His parents report that often when they were driving to the grocery store or the movie theater, Eli would be able to tell them which way to turn to get there. His mother says once when she had parked the car in a large parking lot at an amusement park, she stopped to try to locate landmarks to help her remember what row the car was in and began to verbalize cues. Eli commented, "Why are you spending time doing that? All you need to do is walk out and your body knows how to turn."

In contrast to his very good spatial skills, Eli did not learn how to tell time on an analog clock until he was in the eighth grade. And even now he still gets confused with terms such as "quarter to" instead of "7:45."

Academically, Eli is holding his own and is a solid B student. Even though he is exceptionally bright, he hates to read and finds it a chore. He used to have difficulty on math tests because sometimes he would mix up the details and, for example, add when he was supposed to multiply. He almost flunked math in elementary school and struggled to learn math facts and procedures for basic computation. He still cannot recall the facts automatically but is very good at using a multiplication chart or a calculator. When he entered junior high, he found that math was extremely exciting, especially algebra. He was able to make connections, see relationships, and understand the whole picture. He now loves math and reports that it is his favorite and easiest subject.

His handwriting is nearly illegible, and he types most assignments on a computer using a word processor and a spell checker. When studying, he has found that he needs to convert information into a visual format in order to learn it. He uses mind maps and mnemonics to help visualize the linguistic information and see connections between facts and ideas.

Eli is also very astute at reading people, which is characteristic of a right-brain learning style. He responds extremely well to body language and is frequently able to determine when a person's nonverbal message does not match the verbal message. His parents report that he has always been the first one to notice if someone has a new outfit, even new earrings, or a new haircut. He is also first to notice if someone is not feeling well or is exceptionally tired on any given day.

When Eli talks about his processing style, he states that it has been very useful for him to become aware of how his style differs from the style of many of his teachers and other students in his classes. He reports that learning about how he processes information has helped him to be less frustrated in the classroom, because he can now determine and predict when he needs to perform a task in a slightly different mode.

Sue

Sue exemplifies the type of student who prefers processing information using left-hemisphere strategies. She is currently a senior in high school. She is a very creative student, but when she writes stories, her stories are detailed and sequential and include a great many facts. She places less emphasis on imagination and feeling in her writing than Eli does. She says that she constantly has words floating around in her head. She describes it as if there are little dialogues, even when she is playing sports or just riding in a car. She finds she is constantly reviewing previous conversations or planning future ones. When asked if she ever has music floating around in her head, she says, "Yes, I can make myself think of a song, especially if I know the words really well."

Sue's papers are always very neat, whether they are papers for school or lists she is writing at home. She frequently makes lists, likes to plan, and has charts and calendars in several different places. When she is doing a school paper, she always begins by placing her name in the appropriate position. Her handwriting is neat and the letters are consistently formed. When studying, she likes to make graphs and charts, and she enjoys mind mapping because she can put many details in a simple format.

Sue has exceptionally good skills in reading and spelling. She learned her math facts fairly automatically and easily. She seems to understand math but needs to be very precise and proceed through a problem step by step without any variations. She likes details and needs to make sure she has understood everything before moving on with a problem.

Sue has a keen sense of time. She does not like to be late and is always on time for activities. Her parents report that she is always the first one ready whenever they are going on a family outing. She does not have strong spatial awareness. She struggles to remember where the car is parked, and when she makes a conscious effort to remember, she needs to talk out loud, using such cues as "the third row over from the main door and fourth parking space down." Sue has a very hard time judging the volume of containers. Invariably, if she is putting leftover food away, she picks a container that is too small or way too large. She also has difficulty pouring food into the container and often will spill the food.

Sue enjoys being around other people and is very good at listening. She picks up details when people speak, although she feels she is somewhat weak at reading nonverbal cues. To learn more about how to read nonverbal cues, she reads books on the subject. While doing so, she tries to determine what details to look for to perceive specific nonverbal messages. Her preferred strategies seem to include planning, details, and words.

Lumpers and Splitters

Jane Healy refers to the two processing styles using terminology that avoids the tendency to conceptualize use of only part of the brain.[11] Instead, her labels emphasize the mode of processing. She uses the terms *lumpers* and *splitters*. The lumper tends to perceive information holistically and simultaneously. Using this style, the student lumps all the pieces together. This ability allows the student to design and understand three-dimensional space. Although the lumper is the person whose preferred mode involves right-brain processing, all of us have some lumper skills that enable us to control visual space and understand situations.

The splitter likes to organize information and plan tasks very sequentially. This student likes details and prefers to reason in an analytical manner. He or she likes to put things in order and enjoys automatic routines. The splitter is a person who prefers the left-brain processing style and generally enjoys the analytical, sequential requirements of spoken language. Splitter skills help each person deal with rapidly changing sound patterns, such as phonics, words, and sentences, and fast-moving fine motor patterns, such as writing or rapidly repeated finger movements.

Whole-Brain Processing

By nature, human beings are whole-brain learners. The brain prefers cooperation rather than conflict, and it will work to develop an efficient system that incorporates the two different processing styles. Many of us have our own styles for approaching tasks and problems and our styles depend on the way we mobilize or utilize the different systems of the two hemispheres. Sometimes a specific strategy may be more appropriate for a given task. For example, dealing with details and being very specific and accurate is important for balancing a checkbook, a task that should be organized and sequential rather than global. However, progressing step by step will interfere with activities such as dancing, where it is more important to visualize movements, generalize mental maps, and deal with spatial components of movement fluently and automatically.

For most activities, however, it is important for both hemispheres to communicate and coordinate. To utilize language we need to combine the right hemisphere's processing of prosody and overall meaning with the left hemisphere's ability to deal with details, sequential word ordering, and word meaning. When we meet a person on the street, generally the right hemisphere remembers the person's face while the left hemisphere remembers the name. When we compose poetry, the right side of the brain helps generate the flow of words, the rhythm, and the beat. The left hemisphere deals with the rhyme and the sequence of the words. A creative idea generally arises when our brains coordinate the intuitive, spontaneous, holistic, spatial, and metaphoric functions of the right hemisphere with the logical, organizational, and linear skills of the left hemisphere. Ideas and concepts produced by the right hemisphere alone are frequently nonfunctional until they are tempered by the skills of the left hemisphere.

The ways that students use different processing styles will influence how well they succeed in school. In *LEARN* I explore ways to encourage strategies that typically incorporate right-hemisphere processing styles, and we will use these styles to develop the more left-hemisphere tasks that are required for success in many academic areas.

The LEARN System

Mnemonics are a main aspect of the LEARN system, but I will also discuss other strategies. The overall goal of LEARN is to increase the efficiency of students' learning in the classroom, doing homework, or studying.

LEARN is a collection of strategies that aid recall of information. *Strategies* is the key word because it refers to a *process,* a way of performing or manipulating information. Although using the strategies will usually result in a product, a learned response or outcome, the critical element is the process students use to accomplish the task.

LEARN is not a step-by-step instructional guide. It is a series of suggestions for systems that a teacher may use in teaching new concepts, practicing rote information, or reviewing information. Parents or teachers may also use these systems to help students develop study skills. The goals are (1) to encourage teachers and parents to explore alternative teaching methods and (2) to offer a variety of ways for presenting information. The parent will benefit by using the strategies in LEARN at home and will find useful suggestions for ways to help a student with various homework and memory tasks.

While right-brain styles may be very beneficial for creative and constructional tasks, we teach many of our school tasks and ask students to perform them in a left-brain, analytical manner, using a more sequential processing style. This approach to teaching places the child who prefers an alternative processing mode at a significant disadvantage. Many children who prefer right-brain processing styles may learn differently from those who use left-brain styles, and right-brain children may be labeled learning disabled. Multiple strategies exist that will help children use right-brain processing in ways that will enable them to be successful with the left-brain tasks of the school environment. These strategies will also be very useful to those students who are successful in school, since many children find these strategies exciting, alternative ways to approach tasks.

Some students are very strong left-brain processors, and these students may find that some of the strategies in *LEARN* are actually a more cumbersome way to remember information. For example, such children may be able to memorize the multiplication tables with few repetitions. These children do not need an alternative approach, such as MFM, a math memory technique (chapter 3). For those children, however, who find memorizing multiplication tables quite laborious, a system such as MFM will be extremely beneficial. Some children may also learn the sounds for each letter with little effort. For these fortunate students, a strategy for remembering sound/symbol correspondence is unnecessary. However, there are many children in every classroom who struggle to memorize information and who need multiple reviews. Other children encounter tasks that they feel are impossible to master.

These techniques are also useful for students who use both right- and left-brain processing efficiently because the techniques aid consolidation of memory. The use of more nonverbal and visual approaches will involve students in a right-brain way. Students will also benefit by expanding and developing neglected sensitivities.

I offer various suggestions to help teachers and parents reach and stimulate every child who wants to learn. Since this is a strategies approach, each of these ideas is only a suggestion, a starting point. The creative teacher is advised to take these suggestions and expand them in many ways. A variety of educational therapists, teachers, and parents have used the suggestions included in *LEARN* for many years and at all levels: elementary school, middle and high school, and college. These strategies are effective at all levels because they promote a different kind of learning. They stimulate learning that encourages the coordination between the two processing systems in the brain. Students can apply this coordination at all levels of learning; the only difference is the manner of presentation and the examples used.

An overall benefit of the strategies in *LEARN* is that they combine both visual and auditory processing. Such a combination helps reach the student who prefers to learn through listening as well as the student who prefers to learn through seeing. By teaching a child to combine and integrate both modalities, a teacher can help the student to have a backup system if the preferred mode of memory is not helpful at any given moment.

4M and VIP

My perusal of large volumes of research, articles, and books written on right-brain teaching styles yielded multiple strategies for helping students use this type of processing more efficiently. To coordinate the wide range of suggestions, I organized a system called *4M and VIP*. I designed the system originally to help present right-brain strategies in a systematic way while teaching university classes. The system provides "pegs" to enable a teacher to remember the strategies easily.

The 4M and VIP system involves seven instructional strategies that incorporate right-brain procedures. The first four all begin with the letter *M*: **M**nemonics, **M**etaphors, **M**ind maps, and **M**usic. The last three strategies are **V**isual strategies, **I**magery, and **P**ositive suggestions. I describe these strategies briefly below and in greater detail throughout the book.

Mnemonics

Mnemosyne (/ne-'mo-sin-ne/) was the Greek goddess of memory and mother of the Muses. The Greek word meaning "pertaining to memory" is *mnemonikos. Webster's New Twentieth Century*

Dictionary defines mnemonics as "meant to help the memory; an aid (e.g., a rhyme) to prompt the memory." Mnemonics are clues to help with a memory task. They stimulate spatial and simultaneous strategies that people can then integrate with more sequential strategies. Just as most children learn commercials and jingles rapidly, they will also learn silly mnemonic sentences and will be able to remember them longer. All mnemonics have a pattern that is used to help the students perform a sequential or linear process. The use of a pattern is critical to the success of mnemonics.

In chapter 3, I discuss *Memory Foundations for Multiplication* (MFM), which is a multiplication system using mnemonics. This system provides a way to help children remember their multiplication tables by learning silly pictures and poems combined with a basic memory strategy. For example, *3* is represented by a bee and *9* is represented by a sign. A picture of a bee and another bee is presented with a picture of a sign, or *3 x 3 = 9*. I have been amazed at how fast children latch on to this system and remember troublesome multiplication facts. Children who memorize facts easily do not need additional cues or crutches, but they still enjoy the fun of the mnemonics. For those children who struggle with the multiplication tables, these additional pictorial clues are invaluable.

In chapter 5, I discuss several different patterns and strategies available to help students who have difficulties remembering the words on weekly spelling tests. I discuss mnemonic links for remembering different aspects within words. For example, the sentence "Forty soldiers stormed the fort" helps link the words *forty* and *fort,* which then helps students avoid misspelling *forty* as "fourty."

I present reading, science, and social studies mnemonics in chapter 6. *Memory Foundations for Reading* (MFR) links sentences with picture clues to help students learn sound/symbol correspondence, or which letter goes with which sound. The combination of jingles and pictures helps students memorize key words to use in developing these critical relationships. Once students learn the phrases, they can use the clues to learn to match sounds and symbols and to learn when to use a particular symbol. For example, for the five consonants *t, m, k, f,* and *p,* the related picture sentence clue is "tiny monkeys kiss fat pigs."

Metaphors

Metaphors and other associative techniques provide a link between characteristics of a familiar concept and new information. The learner's goal is to create and then enhance the link between the familiar and the unfamiliar by connecting some common traits. For example, questions that encourage the associative technique are, "What do you do when you're cold? How is that like mercury?" Metaphors and similes are important because they involve processing within hemispheres and they create a synthesis between the activities. I discuss strategies for helping students develop and use associative techniques in chapter 7, especially in content areas such as science and social studies.

Mind Maps

Mind mapping is a technique for organizing information. This method uses visual and spatial strategies rather than the linear strategies needed for outlining. The mind map is an open-ended structure that increases the rapid connection of thought patterns and provides immediate feedback. Mind maps are effective in improving and organizing oral and written language, comprehension, study skills, and the recall of information.

In mind mapping, the central idea is placed in the center of the page, and each subcategory is a branch coming out from the main idea. Other ideas may branch off from the subcategories. This technique allows the mapper to insert information as appropriate. As a study technique, it is important because it helps students organize information visually, which improves comprehension and recall. Students easily perceive the relationship between the parts and the whole.

Students can use the same strategy in written expression or when preparing to write a report. The student organizes the report visually and then writes the report, one section at a time. I discuss this strategy further in chapter 8.

Music

Music, rhythm, and movement are effective techniques that help create a relaxed, stress-free learning atmosphere. They enhance integration of processing strategies and create a link between right-brain, creative, musical, rhythmic information, and left-brain, linear information. For example, language art skills may be strengthened through choral reading or the chanting of spelling words. Other examples include singing multiplication tables or chanting to remember science or social studies information. I present ideas and teaching suggestions in chapter 9.

Visual Strategies

Visual strategies are among the most fun to use when linking right-brain processing to left-brain tasks, and you may use these strategies in combination with any of the other strategies. The old adage "A picture is worth a thousand words" describes this category, which includes picture writing, charting, and cartooning.

Visual strategies use emphasis and exaggeration and may be combined with color, humor, and mnemonics. For example, in remembering spelling words, the tricky part of the word can be emphasized in an exaggerated way. The *i* and *e* in the word *friend* are often tricky aspects and can be written much larger than the other letters and in a brighter color to emphasize the combination. Combining the picture with the mnemonic "A fri**end** to the **end**" helps make this word easier to remember. I discuss visual strategies in chapter 10.

Imagery

Through imagery, visualization, and fantasy, students learn to use their minds' eyes to form visual images. These images strengthen and reinforce learning. Visualization strategies help integrate visual techniques with auditory messages. The strategies link the visualizations to the typically linear information usually taught in school. I present techniques that have a direct relationship to improving academics in chapter 11, methods that help students reestablish a skill that they often lose in our television-saturated society.

Positive Suggestions

This category includes relaxation techniques. You accelerate learning when you provide a relaxed, positive atmosphere and reduce the fear of failure. The right brain is highly influenced by emotions, and the more relaxed it is, the more creative and efficient it is in promoting the total learning process. Positive suggestions include positive affirmations that can be displayed as posters or as tags on desks. I discuss these and other techniques, such as the use of positive self-talk, in chapter 12.

Conclusion

Abigail Adams is said to have stated that learning is not obtained by chance; it must be sought with ardor and attended to with diligence. This sentiment is especially true of children who learn differently from the way we teach. For them, learning is not a process of osmosis. It needs to be worked at, sought, and attended to by use of alternative strategies. The right-brain strategies presented in this book are very useful in helping students be successful in our typically left-brain world.

2

Visualization

Marcel Proust reportedly has stated that the real voyage of discovery consists not in seeking new landscapes but in having new eyes. What a glorious statement about the importance of visual interpretations. Did Proust mean "new eyes" literally? Of course not. What I infer from his statement is that people, especially parents and educators, are able to help bring students to a new level of discovery by helping the students enhance their abilities to interpret visual information. Visualization is one of many tools that can greatly increase this skill.

The Visual Hierarchy

Sight is the ability to discriminate the lighted environment. The Snellen Chart, commonly used in schools to determine 20/20 acuity, is an example of a way to measure sight. True *vision* is the result of students' abilities to interpret and understand, through experience, the information that comes to them through their eyes. Vision is the primary tool through which traditional learning takes place, and often students who have difficulties with vision have limited success in the classroom. Students continually encounter, analyze, and integrate a wide variety of experiences that lead them to visual interpretation. This critical visual foundation is laid through tactile experiences that help link the feel or texture of an object with its visual image. Only when children have efficient interpretative skills do they acquire the prerequisites and lay the foundation needed to benefit fully from classroom instruction and work.

This foundation is critical. It enables students to develop greater efficiency in their work habits and skill development. Although many people go through life with less-than-efficient visual systems, these people may not have reached their full potential, or they may have had to struggle to succeed. When people are not aware that they have a visual problem, they may require extended time on homework, be slow readers, experience blurred vision (especially when fatigued), have to reread information to understand it fully, feel sleepy when reading, or become visually tired in the evening.

Learning is something we do all our lives, and it should be a joyous experience. Reading is a tool for learning, and it should be fluid, fun, and exciting. If a person has to fight to master the mechanical act of reading, then that person cannot experience the joy that comes from acquiring information easily through the printed word. Yet people with visual problems may have had to "plug along" through school, rather than being able to achieve smoothly, quickly, and efficiently.

Today's society is much more complex than it was in the past due in part to the technological explosion. Perceptual demands are great and we need to depend on our visual systems to help sustain visual attention. If the visual system is fragile, it can result in reduced processing speed, inefficiency, and poor quality of work. In today's classrooms there is a great demand for "near-point" work (working at a distance of about sixteen inches from tasks). We are making this demand on younger and younger children. The young visual system is not geared for the continuous stress generated from working at near point, and young children may develop avoidance strategies to disengage visually. These strategies provide a break from visual stress. If a child has other difficulties to cope with, the additional stress and energy needed to contend with an inefficient visual system make learning much more challenging.

Most children may not even realize that their visual systems are stressed. How can they tell? Unlike the language system, in which children are able to compare their performances with those of their peers and adults, the visual system offers no opportunity for children to compare their experiences. How can a child compare his or her own visual experiences with how others see? Children probably assume that everyone experiences the same symptoms.

Experts estimate that vision is an integral part of about 75 percent of the tasks that we require of children in our classrooms. Success in an academic task requires that accurate and precise ocular coordination, focusing, and eye movement skills be established so that the child can process information correctly. The more that children perform these skills with fluidity, flexibility, and precision, the less they will experience visual stress. Table 2.1 illustrates that a majority of students who have classroom difficulties are also experiencing visual skill difficulties. It is based on actual studies conducted by Gerald N. Getman, OD, DOS. Dr. Getman compiled notes of clinical and classroom records of more than 2,500 children, ages 8 to 18, from 1947 to 1980.

Table 2.1. Incidence of Visual Problems

Visual Ability	Percentage by Subgroup			
	Top 1/3 of class	Mid 1/3 of class	Bottom 1/3 of class	Special education

Visually steered and monitored movements
  spatial organization
  knowing where you are
	5	12	20	78

Ocular motilities scanning and locating movements	12	32	65	96
Ocular teaming how well the right eye and left eye coordinate	10	35	65	95
Visual-tactile coordination a match between eye and hand	3	12	20	90
Visual auditory orientations rhythm	5	10	12	70
Near visual focus and attention span staying on task	5	15	40	88

Cognitive imagery
  visual memory
  visualization
	10	50	65	85

Source: Richards, Regina G. *Visual Skills Appraisal: Appraisal of Visual Performance and Coordinated Classroom Activities.* (Novato, Calif.: Academic Therapy Publications, 1984), 10.

It is important to note that even students in the top third of the class experienced some visual inefficiencies. The students were able to compensate for these problems, however, presumably because they did not have other processing or learning difficulties. The students in special education theoretically have the most processing and learning difficulties, and they also have great difficulty compensating for visual inefficiencies. Unfortunately they also tend to have many more visual problems, creating more of a need to compensate, which obviously poses a major difficulty.

The Main Difference
between Acuity and Vision

Acuity is defined in terms of clarity of sight: 20/20 eyesight is the ability to discriminate a letter or object approximately 8.7 mm high (less than 0.5 in.) at a distance of 20 feet. Most children have 20/20 acuity or wear glasses to compensate. The children with such vision problems are usually identified because typical visual screenings done in school identify far-point acuity difficulty; the screenings do not test for near-point acuity difficulty. Most reading demands are at an arm's length or less, so children who have near-point inefficiencies may experience reading difficulties as a result of an undiagnosed near-point problem.

Vision is the result of a person's ability to interpret and understand the information that comes through eyesight. Vision incorporates the ability to maintain clarity as well as many other components. Many children in our classrooms have 20/20 acuity but cannot sustain this clarity for more than a few minutes at a time.

Our eyes require a complex process in order to function efficiently. A useful analogy for our eyes is a pair of binoculars. To get a clear picture, the user must refocus the binoculars each time he or she looks at an object that is nearer or farther away. The closer the user stands to the object, the more effort he or she needs to focus the binoculars accurately. The user must hold the binoculars steady to ensure clarity. The longer the viewing time, the more difficult it is for the user to hold the binoculars steady. The user must focus each side of the binoculars individually, and he or she must unify the two fields to prevent doubling.

This process simplistically describes what happens in *binocular vision*. A person's two eyes must aim and focus in unison, that is, at precisely the same place and at the same time. Such unison of focus allows the person to perceive a three-dimensional world. If the eyes do not focus in unison, the person may have blurred or double vision. Such problems stress the visual system, and a child may try to adjust by covering one eye. When the demand becomes overwhelming, the brain may begin to suppress and in effect shut off the vision to one eye intermittently as a survival tactic. Some symptoms that may result include

- the child easily loses his or her place when reading
- the child sees double or has blurred vision

• the child experiences visual fatigue
• the child experiences visual stress
• the child's visual attention span is decreased
• the child grips a pencil very tightly, indicating she or he is feeling tense due to stress

When children use both eyes in unison, they can maintain clarity easily and without visual stress; they experience true *visual attention*. They are able to devote much more of their energy and attention to the acquisition of meaning and to the academic task at hand. On the other hand, daydreaming, inattention, and acting out are all possible consequences of visual distress that children may be experiencing when they cannot scan words on a page or see the print clearly for an extended time. This stress interferes tremendously with children's ability to learn easily and efficiently. If children are compensating for any other learning difficulty, the visual skill inefficiencies will greatly compound the problem.

As implied in the binoculars analogy, students' eyes must have a high level of control. Without accurate and efficient eye movements, students will not be able to scan a page for information and will generally read aloud in halting voices, read without rhythm, leave out words and word endings, and lose their places. Such children may also experience poor copying skills, visual-motor integration deficiencies, and writing problems. If you suspect a student has visual skill inefficiencies, you might want to use one of the simple tests available to help screen for visual skill efficiency. See Richards's *Visual Skills Appraisal* and *Classroom Visual Activities* for further information on screening for a variety of skills.[1] Garzia and Richman's *Developmental Eye Movement Test,* which tests the eyes' ability to move from word to word and sentence to sentence, is available if you want to test the locating eye movements, technically called saccades.[2] The test also provides standard scores and percentiles, statistics necessary in special education.

Many people often call vision an "act." But optometrist Albert Sutton states that vision is also a "process" that includes all the mechanisms used for acquiring knowledge: "It involves an ability to manipulate the visual space world generated, at first, by the stimulation of the visual receptors. But for understanding and meaning, vision must be integrated with all other sensory and motor modalities of the total body."[3] Dr. Sutton is saying that vision does not act alone. It depends upon and integrates with all of the other sensory systems.

An Optometrist's View of the Development of Visualization[†]

Visualization is a strategy that involves internal knowledge, visual imagery, and, in its more sophisticated forms, visual thinking, creativity, and problem solving. Visualization develops in steps, along a developmental hierarchy that begins when we learn to match visually the internal understanding of our bodies with our bodies' boundaries. For example, if we step from a curb that is several inches taller or shorter than we expected, we would either step down too hard or trip.

Visualization evolves as people develop. Children's internal representations of themselves tell them the length of their arms and legs. When infants initiate visual contact with their hands and demonstrate the ability to control the wiggling of their fingers, they begin to understand where their bodies end and the external world begins. As infants learn to look back and forth from one hand to the other, they progress further along the visualization hierarchy and develop the eye movement skills that will be the foundation for visual inspection, scanning, and organization, so basic to deriving meaning from a lighted world.

Infants next begin to understand that shapes are constant. Initially, they associate only the nipple of a bottle with a good taste and a full stomach. They soon learn to recognize a bottle filled with milk from any angle and associate any aspect of the bottle with a good taste and a full stomach.

Shape constancy is a prerequisite to form perception, which is the basis upon which language is founded in the sighted individual. Infants collect concrete visual banks of objects for which they will eventually recognize the symbolic words; they come to know that there are names associated with all that their eyes see. The person that feeds them is "mama" or "dada" and the round colorful object is a "ball." They will eventually learn to differentiate between similar objects, that is, volleyballs from tennis balls.

Visualization develops further as infants gather experiences by interacting multisensorally with the world. As infants smell, mouth, touch, manipulate, and observe objects as being separate from themselves, they begin to remember an object even when it is out of view. Piaget termed this emergence of memory "object

[†] This section was written by Beth Ballinger, OD, COVD.

permanence." Infants continue to develop and elaborate their memory when they begin to creep and crawl. As long as infants can retain the image or memory of a parent or other center of importance in their world, their new mobility will encourage exploration. As the image of a parent fades, infants will come back and renew the memory and then return to more elaborate explorations for as long as they can sustain the renewed memory.

Many stages in life and development can cause a mismatch between our internal understanding and our bodies' boundaries. For example, during puberty, children's rapid growth causes a mismatch between the internalized image of their bodies and their bodies' real limitations. Children may over- or underestimate the distance to an object and may appear clumsy or accident prone. Pregnant women's bodies also change faster than the women's internal images. Their centers of gravity, all motor activities, balance, and orientation are "off."

One aspect of visualization involves the ability to reconstruct internal mental pictures of a spatial representation without a visual input. This ability exists before the development of verbal language. In its fullest meaning, visualization is the application of visual imagery without internal verbalization for the purpose of propagating visual analytical thinking.

The storage and recall of past visual experiences are closely associated with visualization and visual information processing. Scores from tests that assess visual recognition or visual recall ability may not truly reflect a person's ability to use a visual strategy. An individual may be using a tactile strategy, such as tracing the picture to be remembered with the finger or nose, or a verbal strategy, such as subvocalizing or saying the name of the picture internally. We must evaluate the process of how one is recalling the information to understand the product or score of the test. If children have not developed the ability to create and manipulate visual memory, their understanding of word problems in math or comprehension in general may be compromised. That is, if children have to "wrestle the words off the page" when they read silently, they may have more difficulty comprehending than if someone reads the passage to them.

In order to understand the impact of visualization on reading and spelling, we must understand the mechanics involved with the auditory/verbal and visual systems. Two components comprise the auditory/verbal system: phonic attack, which is the ability to decode letters that are visually presented, and auditory/verbal sequential memory, which is auditory imaging derived from internal recall without an existing visual stimulus. A person can have a good phonetic strategy and have poor auditory/verbal sequential ability, but a poor phonetic attack strategy usually goes hand in hand with poor auditory/verbal sequential memory.

The visual system components that contribute to the processing of language information are comprised of visual recognition, which is comparing a visual stimulus to a memory of a reconstructed internal image based on past experience, and visual recall, which is retrieving a past experience and a visual memory when no visual stimulus is presented. Although visual recognition and visual recall involve internal imagery, they differ in that visual recognition is more basic than recall, and recognition is usually accomplished on a more unconscious level. A person who has good word recognition abilities may not have good visual recall, but a person with good recall ability usually has good visual recognition.

Reading performance is based on the ability of the individual to recognize or recall whole word parts from previous visual memory and the ability to sound out whole words or word parts based on individual letter sounds (the phonic aspect of word analysis). Some individuals may use either a visual or auditory verbal strategy, but a combination of both strategies is more desirable. Spelling performance is based on the individual's ability to reconstruct an internal mental image and then to recall a word or a word part visually without external visual input. Spelling performance is also based on the individual's ability to recall a past auditory sound sequence through the long-term auditory/verbal sequential memory strategy. Again a combination of both strategies is desirable.

By understanding the underlying components of spelling and reading tasks and the students' academic strengths and frailties, we have a better idea of how to build and develop appropriate strategies. Several areas of study require that students use more appropriate visual abilities and visualization skills.

We, as a society, need to nurture creativity and fantasy in our children and ourselves. We need to encourage children as well as adults to see with their own sense of humor, because humor and creativity come from a common root. We need to encourage children to pretend and exercise their own "sense of wonder" because pretending and wonder are the building blocks of visualization, and because imagination is the laboratory in which the ideas of humans are developed. Yet research has shown that although 95 percent of the children entering first grade might be considered creative, by the time these same children get to the fourth grade, only 10 percent are using their creative talents. Modern toys that do everything for the child and excessive television, which encourages a passive mind set, help curb creativity.

Visualization in Learning

Visual skill development is critical because it provides some very important stepping stones for the development of the highest process of visual skill—the process of visualization. Many children do not develop an adequate visualization system because they have not learned many basic visual abilities. Optometrist Homer Hendrickson explains, "Visualization is the result of many prior experiences [movements] of the human organism *matched with what is seen* during these experiences. Some children do not match [integrate or associate] what they feel or do with what they see because they have not learned to align and maintain alignments of the eyes on what they are feeling or doing while they are doing it."[4] And, as Dr. Getman has noted, a student's ability to visualize is necessary for academic success: "The look of a word and the feel of a word are both necessary for an A grade on a spelling paper."[5]

All learning, to some degree, involves a component of imagery or visual knowledge, no matter how slight. Sometimes the individual may not recognize imagery or may use it inefficiently. But true visual imagery is an integrative factor in the efficient performance of language arts, especially reading and spelling. Students can also extend visual imagery easily to science, social studies, and areas of humanities. All of the strategies presented in *LEARN* involve visualization. I discuss specific techniques in each chapter.

Testing for whether or not children use imagery or visualization is different from other testing. It is not the same as looking for use of a procedure or development of a skill. Visualization is a *process,* a way of analyzing information to go from point A to point B. Presenting visual imagery or visual memory tasks alone will not provide insight to the *process* children use to progress through the task to arrive at the output. You need to establish *how* children obtain their answers by asking them to describe

27

how they remember information. Following are examples of questions that will encourage such descriptions:

- How did you remember that ___?
- How did you do it?
- Did you "see" the representations of the form in your mind?
- Did you label it in your mind?
- Did you describe it to yourself?
- Did you both see it and describe it?
- Can you manipulate your object?

The answers to these questions will determine the extent to which a child has used visual imagery. They will also determine if a child has utilized key words to remember different situations. Such questions will provide you with insight to the strategies the child may already be using and will also help you to decide which new strategies you will introduce. Remember that there is no one right answer and there is no one correct way to visualize information.

Following is an excerpt from a song on Harry Chapin's album *Living Room Suite* that beautifully illustrates the message that there is no one right way to visualize or imagine information.[6] Chapin sings about a little boy who goes to school and uses different colors to draw all over his paper. The teacher says,

> It's not the time for art, young man,
> And anyway flowers are green and red.
> There's a time for everything, young man,
> And a way it should be done. . . .
> There's no need to see flowers any other way
> Than the way they always have been seen.

The boy explains that there are so many colors all around him—in the rainbow, in the sun, in flowers—and he says, "and I see every one." The teacher becomes upset and puts the boy in a corner, saying,

> It's for your own good,
> And you won't come out 'til you get it right.

The boy finally gives in and paints his flowers only red and green. He then moves to another town and continues his new habit of painting only in red and green. When his new teacher asks him why, he responds,

> Flowers are red; green leaves are green.
> There's no need to see flowers any other way
> Than the way they always have been seen.

What a sad commentary on how teachers can be inflexible and crush creativity. We need to be flexible about how children can use their visual imagery and visualization skills. We need to think of and use many techniques to encourage variety in these skills.

One Visualization System

One very popular mnemonic system that utilizes visualization extensively is the peg-word system. It establishes key words that serve as "pegs" to aid recall. This technique begins with a code that associates a series of numbers with concrete items that students can visualize. Sequencing and rhyming make recalling these associations easier. The associations become the pegs on which the items to be remembered are "hung." Students can use these pegs to remember a wide range of lists and tasks.

You can play games with children to show them how to use the peg-word system. Following is a list of pegs and rhymes that will be helpful with other strategies within the LEARN system:

1. sun
2. shoe
3. bee
4. door
5. hive
6. ticks
7. Kevin
8. gate
9. sign

I have provided pictures of each of these pegs in Appendix A.

I recommend that you teach the pegs as a game. Pacing is important, and you should keep the pace fairly rapid. You can hold up the pictures or convert them to overheads so they are larger. An example of a possible dialogue follows:

> *Teacher:* Today we are going to play a game to help us remember pictures and relate them to a given number. Here's the first picture. (Display picture of sun.) It is number 1. For number 1, we will remember sun. Notice that "one" rhymes with "sun." Everybody, number one is . . .
>
> *Class:* Sun.
>
> *Teacher:* Number 2 is shoe. (Display picture of shoe.) Notice how the words rhyme. So every

time I say number 2, you will get a picture in your mind of this shoe, and you will say . . .

Class: Shoe.

Teacher: Okay. (Display picture of sun.) When I say number one, you say . . .

Class: Sun.

Teacher: (Show picture of shoe.) When I say number 2, you say . . .

Class: Shoe.

Teacher: (Do not display a picture this time.) To review, 1 is . . .

Class: Sun.

Teacher: 2 is . . .

Class: Shoe.

Teacher: (Show picture of bee.) Number 3 is bee. Everybody get a picture in your mind of a bee. Your bee can look like the bee in this picture, or you can think of your own bee. Does everybody have a picture of a bee? Number 3 is . . .

Class: Bee.

After you introduce each new picture with a number, review all the previous picture and number connections. When you begin, review the numbers in sequential order. As students begin to link the number with the visual image automatically, you no longer need to use the pictures and should begin to review the numbers in random order. Keep the pace of the lesson fast to help the children visualize the pictures automatically.

Continue the lesson, introducing as many numbers as the students can handle. For younger students, introduce only numbers 1 through 5 initially, adding a new number every lesson. For older students and adults, you can introduce all nine numbers in the initial lesson.

Some students may want to create number-object associations for the numbers greater than 9, as well, such as hen for 10, heaven (clouds) for 11, shelf for 12, and so forth. Other students may prefer to use combinations of the first nine numbers to represent a two-digit number. For example, sun and shoe would be 12. Still others prefer to develop additional mnemonics only for the tens, such as hen for 10, plenty for 20, dirty for 30, warty for 40, gifty (a wrapped gift) for 50, witchy for 60, heavenly for 70, matey (a pirate) for 80, and pine-T (pine tree in the shape of a "t") for 90. Select the system you are most comfortable with and that is most relevant to your students' needs.

You should review the numbers and the associated visual images several times to be sure that students automatically visualize the picture for each number. Some students will learn the system almost immediately, while other students will need several review lessons. Once most students automatically make the associations, then you can play games to encourage students to memorize a series of unrelated objects.

Grocery List Game

Introduce the grocery list game by telling students that you are going to show them how to remember a list of unrelated objects. Your students will be able to use this "magic trick" to amaze their parents and friends. Start by giving the students a list of five grocery items to remember. As the students' skills increase, expand the list. To start, I use milk, butter, eggs, lettuce, and bread as my five items. The students can use the peg-word system to connect the items in sequence by making a bizarre visual association. Encourage children to develop their own pictures in their heads, and frequently ask them, "Can you see it?" or "Can you see that picture?" A sample dialog follows.

Figure 2.1. "Yes, 2 is shoe. The butter is melting in the shoe."

Teacher: Our first item is a carton of milk. Number 1 is sun. Get a picture in your mind of a sun. Then visualize the sun combined with milk in some way. Maybe the rays of the sun have become bottles of milk, or perhaps the sun is in the shape of a large, shining carton of milk. Do you have a picture? See the sun with its rays of milk bottles or whatever your picture is. (Pause)

Item 2 on our shopping list is butter. Number 2 is . . .

Class: Shoe.

Teacher: Can you picture the butter inside a shoe? It might be a tub of butter in the shoe. Or maybe the shoe is stepping on a stick of butter. Whatever works for you. Can you see it? Picture it. Visualize it (see figure 2.1). (Pause) Number 1 is . . .

Class: Sun.

Teacher: Our picture is . . .

Class: Milk.

Teacher: Number 2 is . . .

Class: Shoe.

Teacher: Our picture is . . .

Class: Butter.

Teacher: Right. One is sun. It reminds us of milk. Two is shoe and it reminds us of . . .

Class: Butter.

Teacher: Right. See the shoe filled with butter. Item 3 is eggs. Our picture is bee. You might picture an egg with lots of bees on top of it. Or maybe some bees carrying an egg. Can you picture the egg and bees? See it. Hear it. (Pause) Okay, number 3 is bee. It reminds us of . . .

Class: Egg.

Teacher: What do you see?

Class: Lots of bees on top of the egg (or some other appropriate response).

(Review all the associations you have made: 1, sun, milk; 2, shoe, butter; 3, bee, egg.)

Teacher: Now we're ready to do number 4. Our picture for 4 is . . .

Class: Door.

Teacher: Right. Four is door. Our item is lettuce. Can you see a door with lettuce on it? Maybe you see lettuce all over the door. Maybe you see a door with a big handle that looks like a head of lettuce. Or maybe you see a head of lettuce with a door in it. Can you see it? Picture it.

(Review numbers 1 through 4.)

Teacher: What is our picture for number 5?

Class: Hive.

Teacher: Good. Five is hive. Our item is bread. Can you see a loaf of bread sticking out of the beehive? Or a beehive in the shape of a loaf of bread? See it. Picture it. Five is hive and our word is . . .

Class: Bread.

When you have finished introducing all the items, review them. After your students seem to make the associations fairly automatically, state only the number and have the students call out the object. For example, "1 . . . milk; 2 . . . butter; 3 . . . eggs; 4 . . . lettuce; 5 . . . bread." When students do so automatically, call out the numbers in random order.

As students become more proficient in these activities, have them take turns making up lists to be memorized. They may work in groups and should be encouraged to develop their own pictures so that the associations will be more meaningful to them and easier to remember.

Elliott B. Forrest has stated that there are really no people who are poor as visual imagers, there are only people that are "non-utilizers."[7] As teachers and parents, we can encourage children to be more efficient utilizers of visual imagery and visualization techniques. Encourage students to play the memory game at home with parents and friends. Students will enjoy the challenge and will become proud of their skills.

3

Memory Foundations for Multiplication

Learning multiplication tables is a very sequential activity that requires significant efficiency in memory skills. In a typical classroom setting, many children are able to develop multiplication skills through repeated drill and practice. Acquiring these skills is difficult for many other students, however, especially for those who prefer a "lumper" strategy. Research has indicated that students with learning disabilities often have difficulty memorizing basic multiplication facts and they perform less well than their peers.[1] These children and others need something more than drill and practice—they need a strategy to enhance their ability to make the connections, to learn, and to remember. Memory Foundations for Multiplication (MFM) facilitates learning of the multiplication tables through a system of mnemonics. It supplements the general classroom approach and is useful in many of the following situations:

• when you are first presenting multiplication facts to students

• when you are presenting multiplication facts to students with learning difficulties

• when you need a remedial approach for students struggling with traditional techniques

• when you want a creative approach to learning facts for all students

MFM is much more fun and effective if students know the basic peg-word memory strategy delineated in chapter 2. Some teachers prefer to omit the games and start using the peg-word strategy with basic academic associations, and their students benefit from MFM and learn the critical associations with daily review. Most teachers who have used MFM, however, believe that teaching the peg-word system through games saves substantial review time. Using the strategy in a playful way first increases students' motivation to learn it; students may feel more pressured if they realize they are learning the strategy for an academic reason. Chapter 2 will help students memorize the basic strategy and use it in a game, a magic trick, or as a whimsical tool before they use it to learn multiplication.

Prerequisites

Students must develop some basic concepts regarding multiplication before spending too much time on learning the multiplication tables. Otherwise, they develop *splinter skills,* or skills that are learned outside the developmental hierarchy. Students usually learn such skills for a specific situation, but they have great difficulty generalizing the skill or concept to a related situation. For example, a student may be able to recite the 3s table in order but be unable to compute a problem out of sequence or in reversed order (4 x 3 rather than 3 x 4).

Following is a list of concepts that students need to develop before beginning to understand multiplication:

• Place value
• Addition is increasing the value of the number (the number becomes larger)
• Subtraction is decreasing the value of the number (the number becomes smaller)
• Multiplication is a form of addition (3 + 3 + 3 is the same as 3 three times, or 3 x 3)

To be successful with the concept of multiplication, the student should also demonstrate successful mastery of the following skills:

• The ability to sequence random numbers, at least up through five digits
• The ability to represent an addition problem using manipulatives such as Cuisenaire rods, Multi Links, or other objects[2]
• The ability to represent a subtraction problem using manipulatives such as Cuisenaire rods, Multi Links, or other objects

• The ability to set up and represent a multiplication problem using manipulatives, indicating understanding that multiplication is the repeated adding of equal groups

• The ability to reverse the multiplier order of a problem (2 x 3 and 3 x 2) and understand that the answer remains the same

The System

When students begin to learn the MFM system, they must be persuaded that learning multiplication facts is not an overwhelming task. There are one hundred basic multiplication facts involved in learning the tables for 1 through 10, and many students feel they need to memorize all one hundred. You can, however, reduce the one hundred facts to twenty-one by eliminating those that are easily learned and combinations that are reversible. You can illustrate the eliminations on the chalkboard. First, copy the following chart on the board:

x	1	2	3	4	5	6	7	8	9	10
1	1	2	3	4	5	6	7	8	9	10
2	2	4	6	8	10	12	14	16	18	20
3	3	6	9	12	15	18	21	24	27	30
4	4	8	12	16	20	24	28	32	36	40
5	5	10	15	20	25	30	35	40	45	50
6	6	12	18	24	30	36	42	48	54	60
7	7	14	21	28	35	42	49	56	63	70
8	8	16	24	32	40	48	56	64	72	80
9	9	18	27	36	45	54	63	72	81	90
10	10	20	30	40	50	60	70	80	90	100

It is easy to see that there are 100 multiplication facts. The first question to ask the students is, "Do we need to memorize the 1s facts?" The children should, through discovery, realize that there is no need to memorize the 1s facts because the product of any number and 1 is that number. Once they realize that fact, you can erase the "1" row and the "1" column, as has been done in the chart on the next page:

x	1	2	3	4	5	6	7	8	9	10
1										
2		4	6	8	10	12	14	16	18	20
3		6	9	12	15	18	21	24	27	30
4		8	12	16	20	24	28	32	36	40
5		10	15	20	25	30	35	40	45	50
6		12	18	24	30	36	42	48	54	60
7		14	21	28	35	42	49	56	63	70
8		16	24	32	40	48	56	64	72	80
9		18	27	36	45	54	63	72	81	90
10		20	30	40	50	60	70	80	90	100

There now remain only eighty-one facts to be learned. The next question to ask students is, "Do we need to memorize the 2s facts?" The answer is that we really do not need to memorize the 2s facts because we can count by 2s to find the answer. In other words, 3 x 2 is the same as counting by 2s three times (2, 4, 6) or the same thing as adding three two times (3 + 3). It is very important at this stage to make sure that each student understands this basic concept of multiplication. If any student is having trouble with this basic concept, return to the prerequisites and reteach those concepts. Once students realize that they do not need to memorize the 2s tables, you can erase the "2" column and the "2" row as has been done in the chart below:

x	1	2	3	4	5	6	7	8	9	10
1										
2										
3			9	12	15	18	21	24	27	30
4			12	16	20	24	28	32	36	40
5			15	20	25	30	35	40	45	50
6			18	24	30	36	42	48	54	60
7			21	28	35	42	49	56	63	70
8			24	32	40	48	56	64	72	80
9			27	36	45	54	63	72	81	90
10			30	40	50	60	70	80	90	100

Sixty-four facts remain for students to learn. The next question to ask is, "Do we need to memorize the 5s tables?" Most students learn to count by fives when they are learning to tell time on an analog clock. Counting by fives is reinforced when children learn about money and are able to count a group of nickels. If they have not reached this point, it is important to teach them these skills. They need to be able to conclude that by counting by fives you can find the answer to any of the five facts. For example, to discover the answer for 6 x 5, one needs only to count "5, 10, 15, 20, 25, 30." You can erase the "5" row and the "5" column because these facts do not have to be memorized:

x	1	2	3	4	5	6	7	8	9	10
1										
2										
3			9	12		18	21	24	27	30
4			12	16		24	28	32	36	40
5										
6			18	24		36	42	48	54	60
7			21	28		42	49	56	63	70
8			24	32		48	56	64	72	80
9			27	36		54	63	72	81	90
10			30	40		60	70	80	90	100

Only forty-nine facts remain. The next question to ask is, "Do we have to memorize the 10s facts?" There are many "tricks" for determining the product of any number times ten, especially single digit numbers. One such way is counting by tens. For example, to find the product of 3 x 10, you merely need to count "10, 20, 30." Students should also realize that to multiply by 10 they need only put a zero at the end of the number. For example, 5 x 10 = 50 and 8 x 10 = 80. It is important that students grasp this concept. They do not need to "memorize" the 10s facts because they can determine the 10s facts easily by counting or by adding a zero. You can erase the "10" row and the "10" column from the chart:

x	1	2	3	4	5	6	7	8	9	10
1										
2										
3			9	12		18	21	24	27	
4			12	16		24	28	32	36	
5										
6			18	24		36	42	48	54	
7			21	28		42	49	56	63	
8			24	32		48	56	64	72	
9			27	36		54	63	72	81	
10										

There are now only thirty-six facts remaining in the chart. The next question is, "Are there any duplicate combinations that we can eliminate? If we memorize 4 x 6 = 24, do we also have to memorize 6 x 4 = 24?" The obvious answer is no; we do not have to memorize both facts. It is vital that students grasp this concept before proceeding. Then you can erase the duplicate combinations as in the chart below:

x	1	2	3	4	5	6	7	8	9	10
1										
2										
3			9	12		18	21	24	27	
4				16		24	28	32	36	
5										
6						36	42	48	54	
7							49	56	63	
8								64	72	
9									81	
10										

Students have only twenty-one facts remaining. The MFM system will deal with these twenty-one facts.

How to Use MFM

Step 1: Review peg words. Review the picture clues for numbers 1 through 9 using the system described in chapter 2. Correct any errors immediately so that each student's learning becomes automatic and efficient. Use a variety of the following techniques to review the pictures and to help students generalize their learning.

• Repeat each number and picture in unison with the class.

• Match each picture to its number and then match each number to its picture, progressing in sequence each time.

• Match a picture to a number or a number to a picture, progressing in random order.

• Use auditory input (name) and verbal response (for example, you say "bee" and the class says "3").

• Use visual input with verbal response (for example, you show the number 3 and the class says "bee").

• Use a combination of auditory and visual input with verbal response.

Figure 3.1. "Bee times bee equals sign."

Step 2: Establish links. Use MFM pictures and poems. (Twenty-one MFM pictures and the accompanying poems, written by educational therapist Judy Love, are in Appendix B.) Cover the poem and show the students the picture for 3 x 3. Ask, "What do you see?" Using self-stick note paper or marking on the overhead with erasable ink, add the multiplication sign (x) and the equal sign (=), as in figure 3.1. Say to the students, "Let's change this picture to numbers. What would that be?" After the students provide an appropriate response, uncover the poem and read the poem with the students. Ask, "How does this poem help us?" Encourage a discussion about the relationship of the picture to the multiplication fact. To help reinforce the poem, give students a copy of the picture and the poem.

Step 3: Use the pictures. Make three copies of each key word picture included in Appendix A. You can perform step 3 using one set at the front of the room as a demonstration for the class. Each child may also have his or her own set at the desk. You will need to decide which approach will work best for you based on your teaching style and the age of the students.

When you begin, have the full picture and poem posted so students can refer to them easily. Remove the picture and poem as soon as possible so that students will begin to rely on their own memories. You may combine the following steps in a single lesson, especially with older students. With younger students, I advise that you focus on only one step per lesson, combining steps as part of the review process.

1. Using individual pictures, read the poem and have students set up the picture sequence by selecting the appropriate pictures and placing them in the correct order (see figure 3.2). If you are working with younger students or students with learning disabilities, use fewer pictures.
2. Set up the pictures on a clear board. While you do so, the students say the poem.

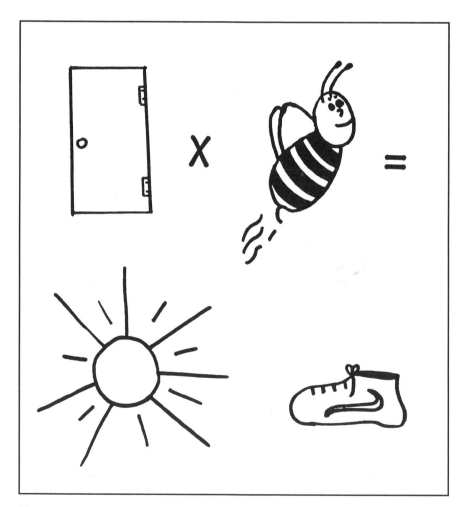

Figure 3.2. "Door times bee equals a sun and a shoe."

3. Students say the poem while arranging the pictures into the correct sequence.
4. Students say the poem while manipulating objects that represent the numbers (see figure 3.3).

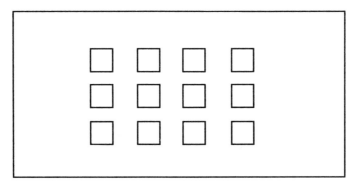

Figure 3.3. Manipulation of rods to represent 4 x 3

Step 4: Review. Review the poems, pictures, and math facts using the sequence in step 3 or one of the following alternatives:

• MFM flash cards. Show the picture representing 3 x 3; students say aloud "9."

• MFM flash cards with poem. Show a fact such as 3 x 3; students say the poem.

• Periodic timed tests, including all facts taught up to that point. When students perform the timed test, encourage them to use the strategy rather than using their fingers. For example, you might say to them, "I'm timing you, but don't rush. When you get stuck, stop, look at the numbers, and try to remember the strategy. You can pull out the poem."

When students take the first timed tests, place all the facts in order. As students advance, begin to rearrange the order of the facts. As students become more proficient in the facts they have learned, add other facts, such as the 1s facts or 2s facts. Have students take each timed test several times. Their initial time would establish a baseline. Each time they retake a test, their goal is to improve *their own* scores. They should chart how many facts they are able to get correct within one minute (see figure 3.4). This visual representation of students' progress motivates them and generates confidence in their new skills. Postpone using the timed tests until students are fairly solid on all of the 3s facts.

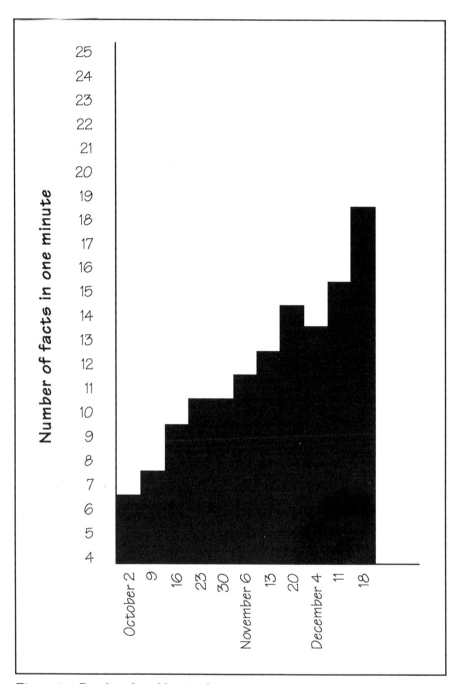

Figure 3.4. Results of weekly timed tests

• Standard math flash cards. Encourage students to answer within ten seconds. Tell them that if they cannot retrieve the answer within ten seconds to go on to the next card. Gradually decrease the amount of time students have to respond.

Cautions and Suggestions

• Use manipulatives such as Cuisenaire rods, link blocks, or counters to reinforce the concept that multiplication is an array of facts. An example of an array for 5 x 3 follows:

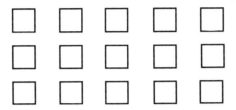

• Discourage finger counting; encourage the use of the strategy.

• Present only two or three facts per session to ensure that students are confident with each poem. For this strategy to be successful, it is important for students to use the poems to come up with the facts within a few seconds.

• Use constant review, cycling through various procedures and steps. Start each session with a review of all facts taught in previous sessions.

• When using the poems, some teachers prefer to omit the tens because they have not taught base 10. Although it is more accurate to use the tens ("3 x 4 is 1 ten and 2"), some prefer to leave it out and just say, "3 x 4 is a 1 and a 2." Poems written for this format are in Appendix B. If you prefer to use the tens, change the last line in each poem to include them. For example,

> Three times four is one ten and a two.
> Three times six is one ten and an eight.
> Three times seven is two tens and a one.
> Three times eight is two tens and a four.

4

Finger Multiplication Systems

The MFM system works very well for many students. Some students, however, may have difficulty with only one or two facts or tables. Others may find the learning of the mnemonics a bit cumbersome. Following are some alternative systems that you can apply and teach as necessary.

Before you use any of these multiplication "tricks," be sure that each student understands the basic concept of multiplication. Students need to be aware that multiplication is an alternative for addition. For example, 4 x 3 means the same as 4 + 4 + 4 or, in other words, a set of 4 three times. You may want to help students visualize the concept by having them arrange objects such as Cuisenaire rods, beads, or other counters. A multiplication grid can also help students understand that multiplication is merely a faster way to add. For example, using the multiplication grid, it is easy to see that 6 x 3 may be calculated by moving down the 6 column three times (6, 12, 18):

x	1	2	3	4	5	6	7	8	9	10
1	1	2	3	4	5	6	7	8	9	10
2	2	4	6	8	10	12	14	16	18	20
3	3	6	9	12	15	18	21	24	27	30
4	4	8	12	16	20	24	28	32	36	40
5	5	10	15	20	25	30	35	40	45	50
6	6	12	18	24	30	36	42	48	54	60
7	7	14	21	28	35	42	49	56	63	70
8	8	16	24	32	40	48	56	64	72	80
9	9	18	27	36	45	54	63	72	81	90

If you are helping students to develop finger multiplication techniques, practice each method until the students can perform the technique automatically. And give students plenty of exercises to help them practice the technique before encouraging students to use it to solve problems with paper and pencil.

Number Patterns

There are patterns in each of the multiplication tables, but many students do not become aware of number patterns automatically. The 9s table, for example, presents a very interesting pattern. To help students become aware of the pattern, write the 9s table on the chalkboard in a vertical column as follows:

$$
\begin{array}{rcrcr}
9 & \times & 1 & = & 9 \\
9 & \times & 2 & = & 18 \\
9 & \times & 3 & = & 27 \\
9 & \times & 4 & = & 36 \\
9 & \times & 5 & = & 45 \\
9 & \times & 6 & = & 54 \\
9 & \times & 7 & = & 63 \\
9 & \times & 8 & = & 72 \\
9 & \times & 9 & = & 81 \\
9 & \times & 10 & = & 90 \\
\end{array}
$$

Point to the column with the products and have the students look at the digits in the 1s place and identify any number pattern that they may see. Then have them look at the digits in the 10s place and describe any number pattern they may see. They may notice that the digits in the 1s place progress in descending order and the digits in the 10s place progress in ascending order.

There are some other number patterns involving nines: It is easy to think of ten more and then minus one. For example, 27 + 9 = 27 + 10 (37) minus 1 (36). This pattern also becomes very evident to students if they look at the multiplication grid that follows. You might also notice that the digits in each answer add up to nine and that the last four answers are the same as the previous four answers, only reversed.

x	1	2	3	4	5	6	7	8	9	10
1	1	2	3	4	5	6	7	8	9	10
2	2	4	6	8	10	12	14	16	18	20
3	3	6	9	12	15	18	21	24	27	30
4	4	8	12	16	20	24	28	32	36	40
5	5	10	15	20	25	30	35	40	45	50
6	6	12	18	24	30	36	42	48	54	60
7	7	14	21	28	35	42	49	56	63	70
8	8	16	24	32	40	48	56	64	72	80
9	9	18	27	36	45	54	63	72	81	90

Students who enjoy tactile cues, and especially students who tend to move and are wiggly in a classroom, may find finger multiplication a very efficient strategy. We have found students use their fingers only as long as doing so is necessary. Once students master the facts, they naturally eliminate crutches, except perhaps to check on specific facts. Some students rely on using their fingers longer than others.

Finger 9s, One Digit

The finger system for the 9s table is relatively easy. Students begin by placing both hands in front of them, on a table, palm side down, with fingers outstretched. The students mentally number each finger starting with the pinky on the left hand (see figure 4.1). You may want to help younger students or students who have difficulty visualizing by placing a numbered circle on the corresponding finger.

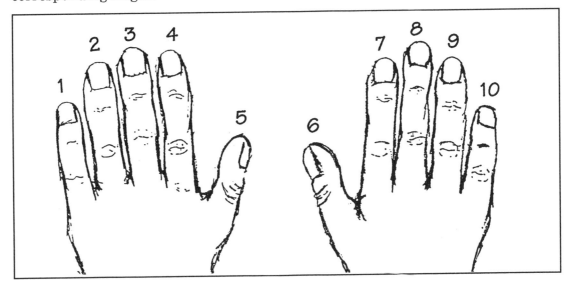

Figure 4.1. Numbering of fingers for 9s

This finger system for 9s works when multiplying 9 by a single digit. If students are multiplying by 5, they would fold in their number five finger, as in figure 4.2:

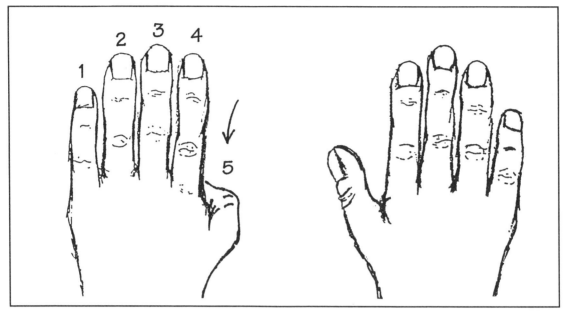

Figure 4.2. Process for figuring 9 x 5

Students then count the fingers to the left of their folded fingers and the total becomes the 10s digit. The number of fingers to the right of the folded finger becomes the 1s digit. Students then have the answer. In this case it is four 10s and five 1s, or 45 (see figure 4.3).

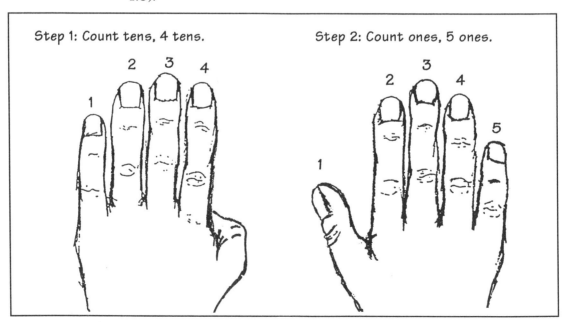

Figure 4.3. Answer to 9 x 5

Have the students practice with 9 x 7. They would put down the seventh finger and then count the number of 10s (six) and the number of 1s (three). The answer is 63 (see figure 4.4).

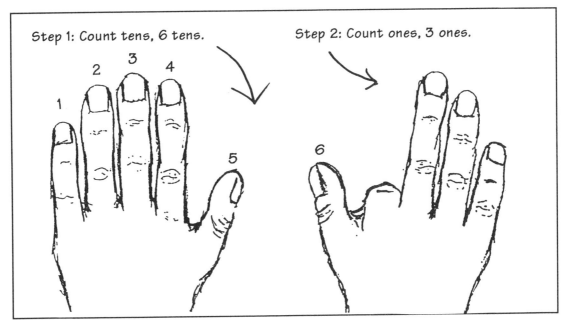

Figure 4.4. Process for figuring 9 x 7

Practice this procedure with all single-digit 9 facts and you will notice how easy it becomes. It also works with 9 x 10, as indicated in figure 4.5.

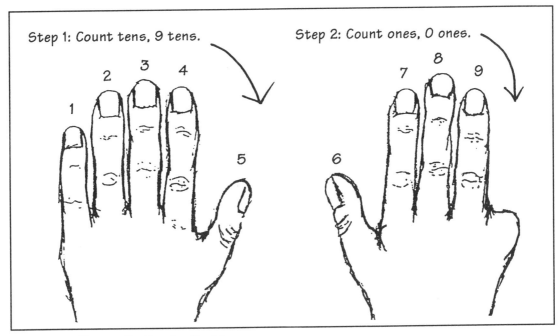

Figure 4.5. Process for figuring 9 x 10

Finger 9s, Two Digits

You can modify the procedure for one-digit problems and use it to multiply 9 by any two-digit number, as long as the first digit is smaller than the second. Place your hands flat on the table, palm side down, with the fingers outstretched. Again, number each finger starting with the pinky on the left hand. To multiply, for example, 9 by 36, first multiply the ones digit (the 6) using the same method described earlier (see figure 4.6).

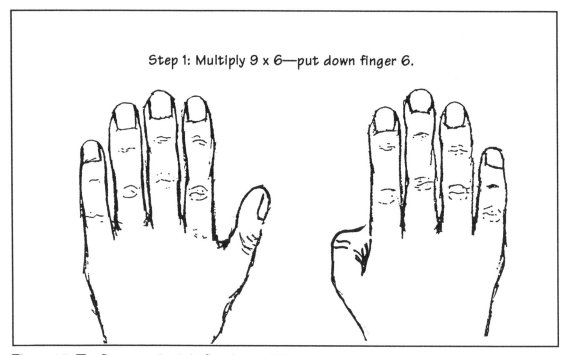

Step 1: Multiply 9 x 6—put down finger 6.

Figure 4.6. The first step, 9 x 6, in figuring 9 x 36

The five fingers to the left of the bent finger represent the tens, and the four fingers to the right of the bent finger represent the ones. Now the 3 in 36 needs to be manipulated. From the left, count three fingers (to represent the 3 in 36). Separate these fingers from the group (see figure 4.7).

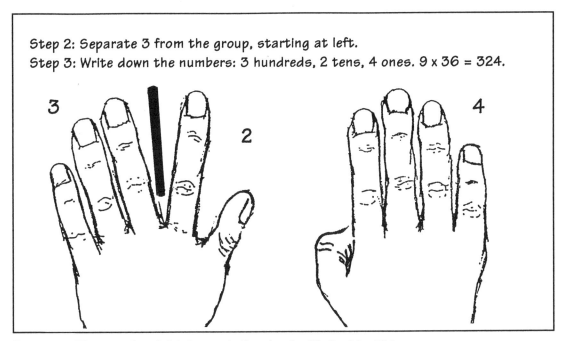

Step 2: Separate 3 from the group, starting at left.
Step 3: Write down the numbers: 3 hundreds, 2 tens, 4 ones. 9 x 36 = 324.

3

2

4

Figure 4.7. The second and third steps in figuring 9 x 36; 9 x 36 = 324

Now there are three groups of fingers: a group of 3, a group of 2, and a group of 4. These groups represent the number 324, which is the product of 9 x 36.

As another example, multiply 9 x 57. First bend the 7 finger, leaving six fingers on the left and three on the right (see figure 4.8).

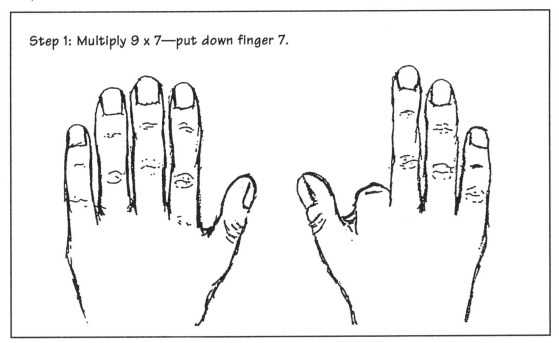

Step 1: Multiply 9 x 7—put down finger 7.

Figure 4.8. The first step, 9 x 7, in figuring 9 x 57

Then separate 5 of the fingers on the left from the group. This results in three groups of fingers: five, one, and three (see figure 4.9). The answer is 513.

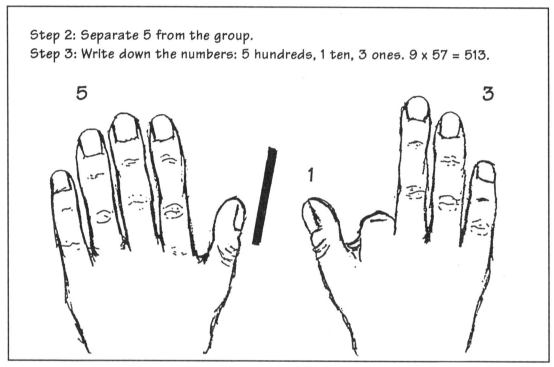

Step 2: Separate 5 from the group.
Step 3: Write down the numbers: 5 hundreds, 1 ten, 3 ones. 9 x 57 = 513.

5

3

1

Figure 4.9. The second and third steps in figuring 9 x 57; 9 x 57 is 513

Remember, the first digit in the number to be multiplied must be smaller than the second.

After the children practice a few problems, you can make a pattern (holding your fingers up or placing them on an overhead) and then have the children determine and write down the problem and the answers represented. This activity will increase the students ability to "read" their fingers and visualize the 9s.

Finger Facts: 6s through 9s

Another finger system, which is slightly more complex than the 9s system, works for the 6s through 9s tables (see figure 4.10).

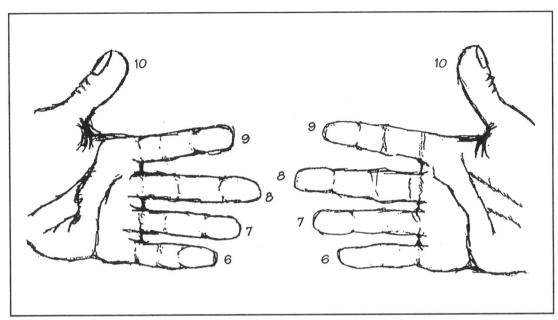

Figure 4.10. Position and numbering of hands for 6s through 9s

To use this system, students place their hands in front of them, with the palms toward them and the thumbs pointing up. On each hand the pinkie is number 6, the ring finger is number 7, the middle finger is number 8, the pointer finger is number 9, and the thumb is number 10. In this system, students will touch together the two fingers being multiplied.

For example, in figure 4.11, the number 6 on the left hand is touching number 8 on the right hand to represent 6 x 8.

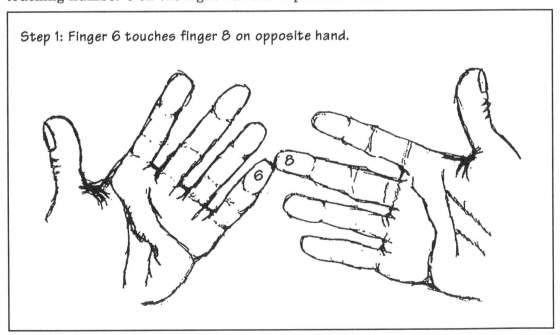

Step 1: Finger 6 touches finger 8 on opposite hand.

Figure 4.11. The process for figuring 6 x 8

The student then counts each finger that is touching or below. In this example there are two fingers touching and two below; four fingers equals 4 tens or 40. In the next step, the fingers on the left hand and on top of the touching fingers are multiplied by the top fingers on the right hand. In this example, 4 on the left hand times 2 on the right hand equal 8, which is the number that goes in the ones column (see figure 4.12.). The product of 6 x 8 is 48.

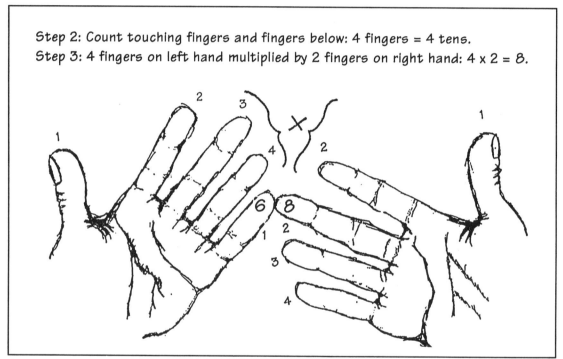

Figure 4.12. Answer to 6 x 8: 48

To try another example, multiply 7 x 8. Notice that the 7 finger (the ring finger) on the left hand touches the 8 finger (the middle finger) on the right hand. There are five fingers that are touching and below, so a five goes in the 10s column. Two fingers on the right hand multiplied by the three fingers on the left hand equals 6, which goes in the 1s column (see figure 4.13). 7 x 8 = 56.

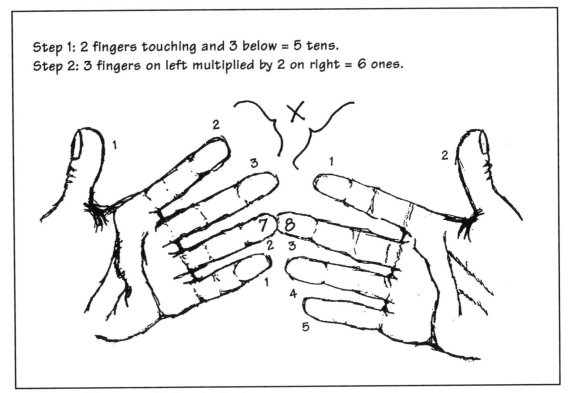

Step 1: 2 fingers touching and 3 below = 5 tens.
Step 2: 3 fingers on left multiplied by 2 on right = 6 ones.

Figure 4.13. The process for figuring 7 x 8

There are two exceptions to this technique that may confuse students. You can remedy the problem easily, however, by writing the numbers on paper. The two exceptions are 6 x 6 and 6 x 7. In 6 x 6, the two pinkies are touching. Counting the fingers touching and below equals 2 tens, or 20. Multiplying the fingers above yields 4 x 4 = 16, so 16 is written with the 1 in the 10s column and the 6 in the 1s column, as in the example. Students would then add these numbers together to equal 36.

$$\begin{array}{r} 20 \text{ tens} \\ + \ 16 \text{ ones} \\ \hline 36 \end{array}$$

Notice in figure 4.14 that the same procedure is used for 6 x 7.

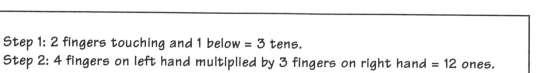
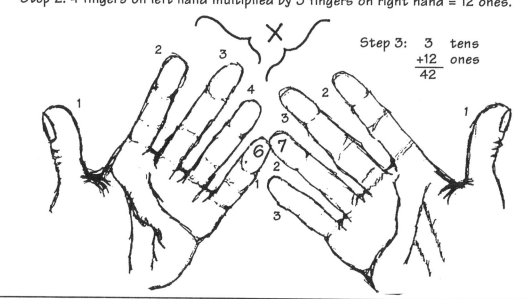

Step 1: 2 fingers touching and 1 below = 3 tens.
Step 2: 4 fingers on left hand multiplied by 3 fingers on right hand = 12 ones.

Step 3:
$$\begin{array}{r} 3 \\ +12 \\ \hline 42 \end{array}$$ tens
ones

Figure 4.14. The process for figuring 6 x 7

With practice, many students become proficient at using these finger techniques, and they seem to enjoy the ease with which they can multiply. Try the techniques yourself and then with your students. You will soon see how valuable it is to have alternative strategies to help students recall facts.

5

Mnemonic Links
for Spelling

The English language is a very visual language, but it is also a phonetic language. It is phonetic because we use the alphabetic system, and sounds are represented by a single letter or letter combination. It has been derived from many other languages, and words derived from other languages retain their visual configurations, such as *ph, mn,* and *y* as vowel sound, creating a large mixture. Anna Gillingham's program is one of many that introduces students to the multiplicity of sound/ symbol associations to help them understand that words come from different language sources.[1] Her program uses the image of the stream of language to help explain this concept (figure 5.1).

Figure 5.1. Stream of language. Reprinted from *Remedial Training for Children with Specific Language Disability in Reading, Spelling, and Penmanship,* 7th ed., 1968, by Anna Gillingham and Bessie Stillman by permission of Educators Publishing Service.

The many different ways of representing one sound can be confusing. The long *i*, for example, is represented in all of the following words but in a different way in each: *silo, sight, psychology, cyclone,* and *cider.* On the other hand, a single combination (ough) can be pronounced very differently, as in the following combinations: *cough, furlough, ought, plough,* and *thorough.* The inconsistencies in English might lead one to spell *fish* as "ghoti" if we used the *gh* in "enough," the *o* in "women," and the *ti* in "notion."

Students should understand basic sound and symbol correspondence and realize that there are irregularities within the English encoding and decoding system. Students also need to be able to remember a given sequence of letters and how they relate to specific sounds. Research has indicated that good spellers use visualization to an extensive degree; they can "see the letters" in their minds' eyes. There are ways to help students visually remember correctly spelled words. The following four steps are very effective.[2]

> *Step 1:* Students trace over (accurately and with fluency) a word on a chalkboard repeatedly, using very large letters. They say the name of each letter as they trace it. This exercise provides multisensory input; the students see the shape, say the name, hear the name, and feel the shape while moving over the letters.
>
> *Step 2:* Students trace the word without touching the chalk to the board while naming the letters.
>
> *Step 3:* Students trace the letters in the air, saying the letters as they trace, emphasizing accurate movements.
>
> *Step 4:* Students repeat the tracing with their eyes closed.

These four steps are very similar to the steps used in programs such as Gillingham's *Remedial Training,* Richards's *Memory Foundations for Reading,* and Slingerland's *Multisensory Techniques.*[3] After a student finishes the steps, ask, "Can you 'see' the word in your mind while you trace the letters in the air?" If the student says yes, he or she is beginning to visualize and to recall visually. If not, he or she needs more reinforcement, practice, and encouragement to see the words in the mind's eye. You can aid students' visualization by asking questions that encourage imagery:

"Can you see which letters are tall?"

"Can you see which letters are short?"

"Can you see the first letter?"

"Can you see the last letter?"

Some English words, because of their unusual or less common spelling patterns, will cause difficulty for students even if those students have a strong foundation in phonetic analysis and a basic ability to recall simple sequences visually. As in other situations, the use of mnemonics can help alleviate some of the problems. Mnemonics work because they help focus on the tricky part of the word and because they provide a link to help the student remember the difficult area.

You must use spelling mnemonics with caution. Presenting a list of twenty words with twenty mnemonics will overwhelm any student. Instead, choose a few words each week and match them with mnemonics to help a student focus on the tricky aspects of spelling. You will help students most by having them make up their own mnemonics whenever possible because they will generalize and use the strategies outside of the direct situation in which those strategies were taught. For example, you may present exaggerated pronunciation to help a student remember a word such as *Wednesday* ("Wed-nes-day"), and students may, on their own, utilize exaggerated pronunciation to help remember the spelling of *together* ("to-get-her").

Creating Basic Mnemonics for Spelling

I use a system of six strategies to help develop mnemonics for spelling patterns:

1. *Mispronounce* the word to help focus on the individual components.

    Wed-nes-day

    To-get-her

    Re-cog-nize

    Mon-o-ton-o-us

    A-ard-vark

2. Create a sentence using a related word that has the same sequence of letters as the target word.

   You **hear** with your **ear**.

   A b**each** is land by the **sea**.

   Use a calcula**tor or** use your fingers.

   The wh**ite** su**ite** is nice.

   It's **ea**sy to work with an **ea**sel.

   Crust-a-**cean** relates to the o**cean**.

3. Create a sentence story that focuses on a specific aspect of the target word.

   Use both i's (eyes) in sk**ii**ng.

   Accustomed: A pair of **Cs** chased us to **Tom** and **Ed**.

4. Create an acronym.

   A rat **in the** house **m**ight **eat the i**ce **c**ream. (arithmetic)

   Balls **a**lways **z**oom **a**cross **a r**oom. (bazaar)

   George **E**aton's **o**ld **g**randmother **r**ides **a p**urple **h**orse—**y**ippee! (geography)

   Rulers **e**at **i**cy **g**rapes **n**ow. (reign)

5. Create a sentence that relates the target word to another word based on its root.

   Large m**usc**les make you very m**usc**ular.

   In**toxic**ation is a very **toxic** condition.

   Knowledge, as we **know**, is important.

   Scholastics are for **schola**rs in **scho**ol.

6. When all else fails, create a comparison that describes the troublesome part in the target word.

   There is no **x** in e**c**stacy.

   There is no **f** in pro**ph**ecy.

   There is no **t** in pre**ss**ed.

   There is no **a** in **eigh**t.

Using the Basic Mnemonics

Once you have looked at the basic patterns, try thinking of some mnemonics for the following words. After you have developed your own mnemonics, see the following section for more ideas. In case you have difficulty, I have included some suggestions following the list.

> Friend
>
> Canoe
>
> Attorney
>
> Prey
>
> Recruit
>
> Tragedy
>
> Comedy
>
> Announce

Suggested Mnemonics for Practice Words

Friend: Look for another word in friend. Create a sentence: A **friend** to the **end**

Canoe: The tricky part is **oe**. What common word ends in **oe** with the same sound? This **canoe** looks like my **shoe**

Attorney: There are two tricky parts here: **orn** and **ey**. Think of words containing those segments and create a sentence: The **key** has **torn** the attorney's shirt

Prey: The tricky part is **ey**. What rhyming word ends in **ey**? Th**ey** like the pr**ey**

Recruit: The difficult part is **uit**. Make a sentence using a rhyming word: The recr**uit** has a new s**uit**

Tragedy: Look for another word within: The **age** of tr**age**dy

Comedy: The tricky part is the middle **e**. Look for another word within comedy: **Come** to the **come**dy.

Announce: Look for other words within: **Ann** weighs an **ounce.**

6

Mnemonic Techniques
for Reading and
Core Curriculum

Mnemonics are valuable for students, no matter what the students' learning styles. Children learn silly mnemonic phrases just as quickly as they learn commercials and jingles, and mnemonics help students acquire new information and recall information more easily. Students who prefer holistic and lumper strategies will relate to the rhythm and jingle of mnemonic phrases and can also lump the connections implied or directly stated in the mnemonic. Students who generally learn without difficulty will find that they can learn rote information at a much faster rate using mnemonics. Mnemonics are effective because they connect the two processing strategies; they integrate spatial awareness and thinking with more sequential information.

Some teachers are concerned that using mnemonics increases the volume of information students need to learn. But you are actually giving the student new memory pathways and a *more efficient retrieval system.* Without a good retrieval system, students can easily forget information that they have already learned. Although mnemonics provide this retrieval system, you must be sensitive to the amount of information that you can realistically present in a single lesson. When students are given too many mnemonics, they may have trouble remembering the mnemonics, just as they had trouble remembering using traditional strategies. But do not be afraid to unleash the power of mnemonics; they have enormous potential and can enhance students' enthusiasm, motivation, and comprehension.

From ancient times, people have used systems to help them remember. The ancient Greeks, without easy access to writing and written material, needed to develop strong memory skills to remember what they had heard. Yates attributes the first formal memory system to Simonides, the Greek poet.[1] Simonides attended a banquet given by a wealthy nobleman in approximately 500 B.C.E. Simonides had composed a poem and dedicated it to the nobleman, and the nobleman wanted Simonides to recite it to him in the presence of the dinner guests. Simonides recited the poem and left. Soon afterward, the roof of the banquet hall collapsed, killing the guests and mangling them so that identifying them was impossible. Simonides was able to identify all the guests because he had remembered exactly who sat where around the table. Because of this event, Simonides realized that arranging things in an orderly way was essential to remembering them, and he understood that mental imagery was very useful in the development of memory. He developed a special technique for training the memory that became known as the Method of Places (Loci). Cicero and Quintilian later used the technique to help their students remember long speeches.

The Method of Places was the first time the peg-word system, described in chapter 2, apparently was used. The principle behind the method is association; you establish a relationship between two things that you can remember easily. Making the relationship bizarre can aid greatly in recalling an image, but there are other factors that also aid the mnemonic association, including movement, connections, and humor. In many mnemonics, the visual mode predominates, but as in the peg-word system, using vision in conjunction with audition can be very powerful.

During the last decade, most of the studies of mnemonics indicate that students who receive mnemonic instruction outperform other students who are taught using traditional techniques. In classrooms using mnemonic techniques, students' grades often improve substantially. Teachers also report that the methods are particularly useful for children who have a history of learning difficulties. Mnemonics provide a tool, a method for retrieving information. Mnemonic instruction also improves children's attitudes toward school and promotes more positive classroom interaction, and it provides a strategy that students often continue using long after they leave that classroom.

The most successful mnemonic techniques entail simple rote rehearsal. Many efficient learners rehearse by rote when they are learning to spell or trying to remember a set of instructions or a series of numbers. Without a hook or a system to integrate the data, however, most people do not retain the information completely or efficiently, which impairs their attempts to retrieve it later.

In this chapter I offer a variety of ideas designed to stimulate creativity. I do not mean it to be an all-inclusive list but a starting point for integrating these strategies into your curriculum. Use these examples as models or samples for expanding your own thinking about how to use mnemonics in reading and core curricular areas.

I use two types of mnemonic strategies in this chapter. An *acronym* is a word that serves as a prompt to remember a series of words in a list. It combines the first letter of each word sequentially. Common examples are **FACE** and **STAB,** both of which relate to music. **FACE** helps students recall the notes in the spaces on the bass staff; **STAB** helps students recall the four voices in a quartet: **s**oprano, **t**enor, **a**lto, and **b**ass. An *acrostic* is a sentence that helps students to retrieve letters in sequence. The first letter of each word in the sentence represents a letter in the list. A common example is **E**very **G**ood **B**oy **D**oes **F**ine; the first letters are the notes on the lines in the treble clef.

Use of Mnemonics with Social Science

You can use mnemonics as a tool to help students study for content areas. Students have fun developing their own mnemonics once they latch on to the system. In geography, for example, students might be learning the locations of the fifty states. If a student is having difficulty learning Iowa's border states because she cannot remember if Minnesota or Missouri lies to the north, you could help her develop a mnemonic. She might focus on the *n* in Minnesota to remember that Minnesota is **n**orth of Iowa and concentrate on the *s* in Missouri to remember that it is on Iowa's **s**outhern border (see figure 6.1).

Figure 6.1. Iowa's borders

Many students, especially in the Midwest, have learned an acronym for the names of the Great Lakes. Each letter in the word **HOMES** stands for one of the Great Lakes: **H**uron, **O**ntario, **M**ichigan, **E**rie, and **S**uperior. To ensure that the word **HOMES** will trigger the correct words, make sure that the students are familiar with the names of the individual lakes. The acronym can serve as a prompt only if the information is familiar.

You can also make the learning of state capitals easier by using mnemonics. For example, for Columbus, Ohio, students may develop a visual image of a little boy or girl waving to Christopher Columbus and saying, "Oh hi, O Columbus." This mnemonic forms a link in students' minds between the words *Ohio* and *Columbus*. Or students might think of the word *pen* for *Pennsylvania* and picture a very hairy pen to recall the city of *Harrisburg*.

Arthur Bornstein, president of the Bornstein School of Memory, has developed a set of mnemonics for learning all of the capitals of the United States.[2] For each capital and state, Bornstein provides a picture with a mnemonic sentence and a poem or brief story on the back. Examples of some of his mnemonics for state capitals include the following:

Little Rock, Arkansas: See the big ARK on top of the LITTLE ROCK.

Sacramento, California: CAL bought a SACK of MEMO pads.

Boise, Idaho: The BOYS watched IDA HOE.

Use of Mnemonics with Science

Medical students and others studying anatomy have used mnemonics for years. For example, many use a common acrostic to help them remember the twelve cranial nerves: olfactory, optic, oculomotor, trochlear, trigeminal, abducens, facial, acoustic, glossopharyngeal, vagus, spinal accessory, and hypoglossal. The mnemonic is **O**n **O**ld **O**lympus' **T**owering **T**op, **A** **F**at, **A**rmed **G**erman **V**aults **A**nd **H**ops. Again, students must know each of the terms; the silly sentence merely helps students remember the sequence and also ensures that no item is left out. If students do not know the names of the individual cranial nerves, however, they would not be helped by knowing the first letter. The value of the mnemonic is its aid in integrating and synthesizing the information that students are learning.

Another common mnemonic helps students to remember the colors of the rainbow and their order. This mnemonic is fairly easy because most students are familiar with the basic color names, with the possible exception of indigo. The mnemonic for the rainbow is the name **Roy G. Biv,** which stands for **r**ed, **o**range, **y**ellow, **g**reen, **b**lue, **i**ndigo, and **v**iolet. Younger students might want to draw a picture of a little boy dressed in the colors of the rainbow to help stimulate understanding and recall.

Students who are studying the solar system must often learn the names of the nine planets in order, starting from the sun. Students can use an acrostic to learn the names, but again, they must be familiar with the names of the planets so that the acrostic merely triggers their memory. The mnemonic is **My Very Earnest Mother Just Served Us Nine Pickles,** which helps students remember **M**ercury, **V**enus, **E**arth, **M**ars, **J**upiter, **S**aturn, **U**ranus, **N**eptune, and **P**luto.

As another example, in your unit on vertebrates, you can encourage students to draw a picture of a farm setting, including a vertebrate from each of the five main classes. They can call their picture **"Farm B,"** providing an acronym to help them remember **f**ish, **a**mphibians, **r**eptiles, **m**ammals, and **b**irds.

Mnemonics with Sound/Symbol Correspondence

Learning sound/symbol correspondence, or which letter goes with which sound, is often easier with a mnemonic system. *Memory Foundations for Reading* (MFR) has mnemonic sentences with picture clues.[3] The combination of jingles and pictures helps students memorize key words to help them develop the sound/symbol correspondence. Once they have the structure, students can use these clues and learn when to match sound and symbol. Colored pictures enhance students' ability to visualize the sentence clues because the pictures stimulate right-brain processing. For example, for the consonants *t, m, k, f,* and *p,* the pictured clue is "**T**iny **m**onkeys **k**iss **f**at **p**igs" (figure 6.2).

Figure 6.2. Picture clue: Consonants t, m, k, f, p

apple **E**d **i**s **o**n **u**mbrella

Eve types,
"Huge snake broke bike"

Figure 6.3. Picture clue: Vowels a, e, i, o, u

Figure 6.4. Picture clue: Final e makes vowels e, y, u, a, o, and i long.

For the short vowels, the mnemonic is "**A**pple **E**d **i**s **o**n **u**mbrella" (figure 6.3).

The long vowels are represented by the picture in figure 6.4, "**E**ve types, '**H**uge **s**nake **b**r**o**ke b**i**ke.'" Notice how the key word for each sound/symbol relationship is represented by a pictured object. This representation helps the students develop a peg to remember the symbol for the sound. Then, when reading or spelling, students can refer back to the association to help trigger the sound they need. When students are able to make these associations consistently, their retrieval systems are much more automatic.

Set 2 in MFR presents multiple sounds for a single letter and is called "This letter (or digraph) makes all these sounds." For the digraph *ch* the students have the picture "**ch**icken **ch**ef washes **Ch**ristopher" (figure 6.5). A picture of "**G**eorge **g**oat" represents the two sounds for the letter *g* (figure 6.6).

In English there are many sounds that can be spelled in alternate ways. It is important for students to learn the word cues that may trigger some of the sound patterns. Before they can learn the cues, students must understand that some sounds can be spelled in several ways. Students should also know some (or all) of the primary word cues. Set 3 in MFR presents this aspect of sound/symbol correspondence and is called "This sound is spelled all these ways." There are eight primary ways to spell the long /a/ sound, and these are represented by two MFR pictures (figures 6.7 and 6.8). There are five primary ways to spell the long

chicken **ch**ef
washes **Ch**ristopher

Figure 6.5. Picture clue: Different sounds of digraph ch

George goat

Figure 6.6. Picture clue: Different sounds of g

baby sprays paint
on the snake

Figure 6.7. Picture clue: Four ways to spell long /a/

hey, eight great veins

Figure 6.8. Picture clue: Four more ways to spell long /a/

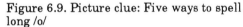

Figure 6.9. Picture clue: Five ways to spell long /o/

Figure 6.10. Picture clue: Two ways to spell /oi/

/o/ sound, and these are represented by a single picture (figure 6.9). Some of the pictures represent a shorter phrase, such as "**oi**l b**oy**," "**f**at **Phi**llip," and "**ch**ef's **sh**adow" (figures 6.10, 6.11, and 6.12).

In teaching a mnemonic system such as MFR, you would overload students if you presented too many pictures at once. The speed with which you present the material will depend on the students' skills and ages. You will learn to pace the presentation based on your own group. It is important that students have ample opportunity to use the new connections they are developing. Just memorizing the sentences without understanding them— and without any opportunity to use and generalize the knowledge—is not very effective. Help students develop and learn the mnemonics. Then give them many opportunities to use the connections. Present many words for them to spell and read using the new sounds. Continually encourage them to refer back to the associations they have developed by asking questions such as "What is our key word?" or "What was that picture with the chicken?"

When you need to present a troublesome sound or a tricky spelling or when you want to reinforce a particular sound/symbol relationship, you will find it is fairly easy to develop a mnemonic for that situation. The trick is to think of a connection between the two items. Drawing a picture (even line drawings) will help you enhance the overall efficiency of using mnemonics. If you cannot

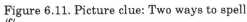

fat Phillip

chef's shadow

Figure 6.11. Picture clue: Two ways to spell /f/

Figure 6.12. Picture clue: Two ways to spell /sh/

draw a picture, create the situation and encourage students to develop pictures in their own heads. For example, instead of "fat Phillip" for the two ways to spell the /f/ sound, you might use a phrase such as "funny phone." The result is the same. The student learns to make a connection between the two ways to spell the /f/ sound.

Mnemonics with Written Expression: PLEASE

A process-oriented approach to writing is often the most efficient road to a good product. Successful writing involves specific cognitive behaviors on the part of the student. The writer selects strategies to complete the subprocesses of planning, writing, and revision. By selecting strategies, the writer takes control of cognitive processes. The writer's awareness and implementation of strategies is called *metacognition* ("meta-" means "knowing about"). Research has demonstrated that students' writing improves significantly when teachers intervene directly and teach metacognitive awareness while teaching the writing process to students.[4]

Metacognitive proficiency allows students to engage in the subprocesses of prewriting, planning, actual composition, and revision. Such strategies, however, are only as efficient as the students' ability to recall and apply each step in the metacognitive process. The PLEASE strategy was developed to address specific types of writing difficulties related to the subprocesses listed above. All writers will benefit from this strategy, but it is even more important for students with learning disabilities or other struggles in academics. Marshall Welch, assistant professor in the department of special education at the University of Utah, has studied children with learning disabilities.[5] He found that use of the PLEASE strategy helped students improve their attitudes toward writing and writing instruction.

PLEASE is an acronym that facilitates metacognitive problem-solving strategies. This mnemonic provides students with a sequence of activities that will help them complete a writing task independently. The letters in PLEASE stand for

> **P**ick a topic
>
> **L**ist your ideas about the topic
>
> **E**valuate your list
>
> **A**ctivate the paragraph with a topic sentence
>
> **S**upply supporting sentences
>
> **E**nd with a concluding sentence and evaluate your work

Encourage students to progress through each step in PLEASE systematically. This helps them think about and concentrate on one step at a time. The result is a high level of writing efficiency, which is definitely "pleasing" to both teachers and students.

Mnemonics with Proofreading: COPS

Once students are efficient in writing their ideas in smooth, coordinated sentences, then learning to proofread is vital. Students derive great benefit from proofing their work in four separate steps because they concentrate on only one aspect at a time. Often when students are asked to proofread, they miss many errors because they are not systematic in their efforts. One proofreading strategy that works well with all students is the COPS strategy. The COPS strategy reminds students to proofread their work using four separate steps. It is another metacognitive strategy because it encourages students to focus on the subprocesses involved in proofreading. The letters in COPS stand for

Capitalization

Organization

Punctuation

Spelling

The overall mnemonic used to help students remember to use COPS is a police officer saying "Police your work!" (see figure 6.13). Students will use cues to help them remember each of the steps. You may need to modify the cues to make them appropriate for your grade level. Keep the cues visible so students do not have to memorize them, but be sure that the students understand each cue. The cues that follow were designed for upper elementary.

Figure 6.13. Police your work!

Capitalization

- first word in a sentence
- I
- specific names (Regina)
- specific places (California)
- specific titles of people (Doctor, Mr., Mrs.)
- specific titles (*Treasure Island,* "The Cosby Show")
- specific days and dates (Labor Day, Friday, May)
- abbreviations (Jr., NFL)
- organizations (Girl Scouts)
- building names (Statue of Liberty, Empire State Building)

Organization

Organization is critical in any written assignment. Students will find it helpful to think of the basic organization of each paragraph before they begin writing, but they will also benefit from looking carefully at the way their thoughts are organized when they proofread their papers. A paragraph needs a *topic* sentence at or near the beginning. The sentences that follow the topic sentence are *supporting* facts that elaborate upon the topic sentence. The paragraph then ends with a *conclusion.* This organization is exemplified by a picture of a dinosaur, which helps the students remember the basic three steps for organization (see figure 6.14). The *top* of the dinosaur represents the *topic sentence* or main idea. The middle of the dinosaur *supports* the animal and reminds students to remember to have *supporting details.* The end of the dinosaur is the *tail,* which represents the *conclusion* or the ending.

Students can use the same sequence to organize an entire paper. The initial paragraph is the introduction, which should summarize or provide the basis for the overall paper. The middle paragraphs are the supporting facts, which elaborate upon the main ideas. At the end is a concluding paragraph, which summarizes the basic ideas or, for students who are more skilled, expresses the importance of the paper.

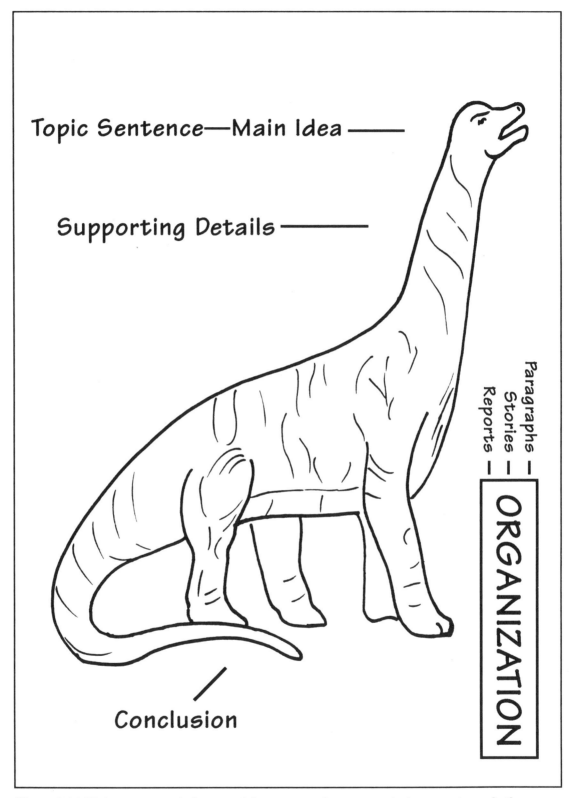

Figure 6.14. Picture mnemonic for organizing paragraphs, essays, stories, reports, and other written works

Punctuation

Although there are many rules for understanding and correctly using punctuation, I have included six of the more important rules here for students to use when they are proofreading their papers. Select the rules you find most important for your groups and put the rules in a place where your students can refer to them easily.

Periods

at ends of sentences (We will go tomorrow.)

in abbreviations or groups of initials (Dec. 3, Calif., U.S.A.)

Question Marks

at ends of questions (When are we going?)

Exclamation Points

at ends of sentences showing excitement or emotion (Please hurry!)

at ends of sentences that are commands (Stop!)

Commas

to combine two complete thoughts (compound sentence) with the words *and, nor, but, yet,* or *so* (Mary and Jay were married last month, and I missed the wedding.)

to join two clauses, the first of which begins with the word *when, because, although, and,* or *after* (After she heard the news, she fainted.)

with an appositive, that is, words that rename something or someone in the sentence (John Brown, the man behind the desk, is a doctor.)

when addressing a specific person (Wanda, will you call me tonight?)

with lists (Tonight we are having hot dogs, beans, and salad.)

after informal greetings in letters (Dear Sally,)

in addresses (20 Stanton St., Dayton, Ohio 68760)

in dates (It happened on November 4, 1984.)

with quotations ("Dad will come later," said the girl.)

with two or more adjectives that each describe a noun (She is a quick, reliable worker.)

Quotation Marks

when someone is speaking (He said, "You are the nicest girl I know.")

with titles of articles in magazines, chapters in a book, songs, poems, TV programs ("Sesame Street," "Yankee Doodle")

Apostrophe

to show possession (This is Mark's dog.)

in contractions to indicate omitted letters (don't, can't, hasn't)

Spelling

Because English spelling is so complex, I recommend that you emphasize only four or five simple spelling rules, depending on the grade level and ability of your students. You can add rules or change them according to your students' needs. The following examples are for the fourth-grade level:

- Short vowels: Apple Ed is on umbrella.
- Vowel + e, the vowel says its own name: name, time.
- Closed-syllable words:

  one syllable
  short vowel
  end in a single consonant

- Closed syllables that end in *f, l, s, z, k,* or *ch:*

  vowel is short
  end with *ff, ll, ss, zz, ck, tch*

The Importance of Teaching Strategies

Strategies are fun, and more important, they are effective. They help students to learn more rapidly and to organize their learning more effectively. Use the examples in this chapter as a starting point, and create your own strategies to fit your teaching needs. You will notice that your students' motivation increases.

7

Use of Metaphors in the Classroom

In *LEARN,* I use the term *metaphor* to refer to a wide variety of associative techniques, including metaphors, similes, and other forms of creating associations. These associative techniques link a familiar concept with new information. Metaphors place an abstract concept within the realm of the concrete. They clarify a concept by using students' experiences.

Metaphors are important because they involve both hemispheres of the brain and synthesize activities. When combined with visual imagery, they develop the right-hemisphere skills of creating links and looking at the whole, which then link with left-hemisphere learning. Your goal is to connect two concepts, objects, or events that are dissimilar by linking them based on a common trait.

Children often delight in the stimulation of insights and feelings that the symbolism and imagery of metaphoric language provide. People have used metaphors in their literature throughout history to help develop or explain a concept. Examples include parables and simple animal stories, including Aesop's fables. More complex metaphors are found in poetry.

Advantages of Teaching through Metaphors

The use of metaphors in teaching is not a new process; good teachers have always helped students understand new ideas by explaining the ideas in terms of something students already understand. Teachers who are aware of right-brain processing have learned to emphasize metaphors so that students can include this valuable tool in their own bag of strategies. But offering students a connection is only the beginning of teaching students how to use metaphors. The connection provides a model, but it does not teach the skill. A teacher must ask students to generate their own metaphors and to discuss those metaphors themselves.

There are many ways to help students develop their own metaphors. Asking students what they know that is similar to or different from the concept being studied is the most direct way. Students who are most skilled at making connections as part of their learning processes benefit dramatically from the use of metaphors. As other students become more skilled in making connections, they will realize that they can learn much more efficiently.

Using metaphors to learn is holistic because it constantly focuses on the process of recognizing and understanding patterns and principles. Each new concept or item is not an isolated set of information but is an opportunity to make connections with what students already know. When you encourage students to compose their own metaphors, you invite them to bring their own experience into the classroom, which increases their understanding and motivation.

Students often have difficulty asking questions that clarify what they do not understand. But their stating "I don't understand" does not tell the teacher what aspect of the concept to explain in more detail. If the student can ask the question using a metaphor, however, such as, "Is a kidney like a coffee filter in how it filters?" then the teacher can explain the similarities as well as the differences between the two items.

Simple Use of Metaphors with Young Children

It's Like

You can encourage young children to think using metaphors by asking them to make comparisons. Accept any comparison. For example, you can have them complete sentences such as the following:

"Dogs smell like _____."

"School is like _____."

"Water feels like _____."

"Green reminds me of _____."

"A bed reminds me of _____."

I Spy

You can also have children play a game similar to "I Spy." Instead of saying, "I spy something blue," however, the children would use phrases such as "I spy something that is like a soft crayon" (chalk) or "I spy something that is used to put papers together" (a stapler).

Innovating on Sentence Patterns

Author Bill Martin uses substantial descriptive language in his *Sounds of Language* series. He suggests that students substitute words in stories. He calls the activity "innovating on sentence patterns" and suggests that teachers aid students' reading by "inviting them into systematic, and at the same time, creative and lively experimenting with various patterns." He recommends encouraging students to transform a sentence by using the structure as a "basis for creating a semantically new sentence."[1] For example, in the following sentence, students could substitute the words that follow for the word *cow:*

I never saw a purple cow.

horse.

pig.

vampire.

This type of "manipulation of model sentences . . . firmly connects language learning with a child's personal use of language."[2] You can create similar activities using any reading material. You need only to focus on a noun, an adjective, or a verb and encourage students to create an innovative sentence by suggesting alternatives for the target word.

Visual Analogies

In this type of activity, you show students pictures of two objects and ask the students to describe the similarities. Encourage them to consider color, material, texture, shape, size, and function. Some examples include

- A sofa and a chair (you sit down on both)
- A pencil and a crayon (you use both for writing on paper)
- A head and a ball (both are round)
- The sky and a blue flower (both are blue)

As a variation, students cut out ten pictures of a variety of items from magazines. They paste their pictures in a vertical line on pieces of paper. Then they go through the magazines again and find pictures that have a characteristic that is similar to a characteristic of each item in their list. For example, if their initial list includes scissors, shoes, a cake, a dog, and a window, they might select pictures that they can pair with the items:

- Scissors and knife (both are used for cutting)
- Shoes and slacks (you can wear both)
- Cake and bread (you can eat both)
- Dog and a cat (both are animals that can be pets)
- Window and drinking glass (both are made of glass)

Use of Metaphors with Older Students

You can use metaphors to stimulate students' thinking about new concepts in content areas. For example, students could define *infinity:* "It's like looking in a mirror and seeing yourself see yourself." Imagine the difference between two groups of students studying the concept of the infinity of space. In one situation, the students look up definitions in dictionaries and find a few examples in textbooks of such facts as the size of the universe and the duration of time. In the other situation, the teacher brings in two mirrors and initiates a discussion of the metaphor as a means of explaining and exploring the concept of immeasurability. The teacher then asks the students to generate metaphors of their own.

The second method is not only considerably more interesting to students, but it is also likely to produce a deeper and clearer understanding of the concept of infinity as something that goes on and on. It helps students grasp the concept in ways that make sense in terms of their own experiences. It challenges them to extend their understanding and enables the teacher to assess how well they understood the concept by the metaphors they offer.

Another way to stimulate students' thinking is to have them compare something they know about with a new concept you are introducing. For example, you might ask your students to compare volcanoes and revolutions. Ask, "How is a volcano like a revolution?" As students brainstorm, write all the characteristics they think of for volcano on the board. Write all the characteristics they think of for a revolution in a different list. Then go through the two lists and encourage students to identify the similarities. Discuss the differences in the lists. This activity helps students analyze the characteristics of both topics.

The following questions will stimulate students' thinking:

- What do you know that is like ___?
- How are they alike?
- How are they different?
- What ___ is like this? (animal/machine/color/cloth)

Linda Verlee Williams has outlined three main steps for using metaphor in the classroom.[3]

1.   Decide exactly what you want to teach and what general principle is involved. (See questions 1 through 4 in the sample planning session that follows.)

2.   Generate metaphors. Select the one that best communicates the concept you've chosen to teach and clarify the discrepancies. The discrepancies are the ways in which the metaphor does not fit the subject. (See questions 5 through 9 in the sample planning session.)

3.   Make a lesson plan that includes how you will elicit metaphors from students. Ask yourself, "How do I put all this together?"

Following is an example of a teacher's planning session to set up a metaphor comparing a coffee filter to kidneys before teaching the metaphor in the classroom. These questions illustrate Williams's steps detailed earlier.

1.   *What do I want students to know about the kidneys?*
     How they function and their importance to the body.

2.   *How do they function?*
     They filter waste.

3.   *How do they filter waste?*

They sort molecules. They allow some molecules to pass through and retain others.

4. *What is their importance to the body?*
   They remove waste from the blood so that the blood can carry more nutrients and pick up more waste.

5. *What can I think of that filters waste by sorting out something or that functions like a kidney?*
   A fuel filter or a coffee filter; different kinds of sorters: a gravel screen, an egg sorter, IBM card sorter; a parking lot where cars with certain stickers are admitted; school games where you need a student card to get in.

6. *All my metaphors are sorters. Do any of them purify a circulating system?*
   The fuel filter does.

7. *Is everyone in the class familiar enough with a fuel filter to understand the metaphor?*
   No.

8. *Ok, I can still use it to clarify things later on. Can I find a clear metaphor to introduce the idea?*
   A gravel sorter. A demonstration with a gravel sorter will show how the sorting works. Also, a coffee filter. I'll have to make it clear that the kidneys don't sort on the basis of solids versus liquids.

9. *How is the gravel sorter different from the kidneys?*
   It's not part of a circulating system. Its sorting is much simpler than the kidneys. The gravel sorter uses the sole criterion of size, whereas the kidneys use much more complex criteria.

10. *How do I put all this together?*

Some teachers have found that students become so interested in the analogies that the students generate too many ideas and begin to bring in topics that are less related. If your students begin to bring up such topics, you *must* sum up by stressing the main point you want students to remember and other significant points that they may have suggested. Use the chalkboard for the summary to provide a visual listing.

Remember that an analogy is never *exactly* like the thing to which it is being compared, and there will always be discrepancies. In developing metaphors for teaching, look for the closest fit possible. The closer the analogy, the less likely it is to confuse your students. However, student-generated analogies do not need to have the same close fit as teaching analogies. Students can demonstrate an excellent grasp of the subject, even with a poor analogy, if they can verbalize their thinking.

Use of TV Commercials

Middle and high school students will enjoy watching TV commercials to search for examples of metaphoric language. Accept any logical example they suggest, because the *process* of looking for comparisons is more important than the actual comparison.

Use of Cartoons, Comics, and Advertisements

Students enjoy cartoons and comics, and you can use cartoons and comics easily to help students begin to look for associative language in real-life situations. Many advertisements also use such language and encourage comparisons between unlike ideas or objects. Encourage students to search newspapers and magazines for comics and advertisements that use language that makes a comparison between two objects or ideas, especially if that comparison is somewhat unusual or unexpected. Students in upper elementary, middle, and high school are generally successful with this activity, but younger students may not be developmentally ready to deal with this aspect of abstract language. Have the students bring in their pictures, comics, and advertisements, and use the pictures as a basis for discussion. Following are examples of questions that will stimulate students' thinking further:

- Which word in this ad has two meanings?
- What is the meaning that you expect when you first see the word?
- What is the second meaning?
- How are these two meanings (or ideas) alike?
- How are they different?

Here are some examples of materials students have brought in:

- An ad sponsored by the California Coastal Commission presented a full-page picture of a variety of brightly colored fish. The caption read "Save Our School" in large letters. Underneath was "adopt a beach."

• An ad for dog food showed a large picture of a turkey holding an ad for "The best dog food in the world." In large letters was the heading "Is your dog the victim of foul play?" The ad then described how many dog foods include duck beaks, quail's feet, feathers, and other "poultry by-products"—all except, of course, the one being advertised, which included only chicken meat, not by-products.

Follow-up Activity

To practice your own skills in using metaphors, think of what animal is like the brain's right hemisphere and what animal is like the left hemisphere. Some examples follow. Do not read the examples until you have tried to think of some answers on your own. The sample answers are only suggestions for starting the thought process.

Sample Answers

An eagle and an ant: An eagle is like the right hemisphere because when it is flying, it is visual and obtains information through its eyes. It gets a large picture as it is soaring over the land. The ant is like the left hemisphere because it sees only one aspect or detail at a time. As it moves along the ground, it can see only the information it passes step by step.

A dolphin and a horse: A dolphin is like the right hemisphere because it has great fluidity of movement and is very social. A horse is like the left hemisphere because it is more linear as it walks along the land and it takes one step at a time.

8

Using Mind Maps
in the Classroom

Mind mapping is sometimes called *webbing, clustering,* or making *topical nets* and is a technique used to organize information.[1] Mind mapping requires a visual and spatial method of organizing information rather than the linear method required for outlining. Mind maps are effective in improving and organizing students' oral and written language and they increase study skills and recall of information. The map pattern allows students to see and represent connections more easily than does an outline. Students can add information to mind maps easily, and because mind maps facilitate making rapid connections between ideas, they help students grasp the whole picture and the relationships among the parts.

In mind mapping, students place the central idea in the center of the paper, and each subcategory branches off of the main idea. Maps are individual expressions of how to organize information; they allow each student to determine the manner most appropriate for him or her. Mind maps can vary from extremely simplistic, as the one shown in figure 8.1, to very complex. Figure 8.2 is an

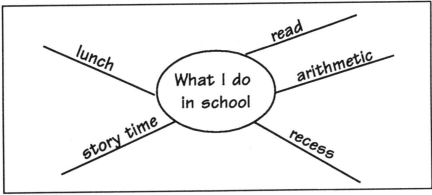

Figure 8.1. A simple mind map

example that is somewhere between the two extremes.[2] I have diagrammed the basic structure of mind mapping in figure 8.3. To make the mind map more complex, students can add additional facts under the subcategories. Students can use a variety of symbols, including arrows, colors, geometric shapes, and codes. They can add information using words or pictures. Some people prefer to enclose the words within circles as illustrated in figure 8.4. Students can explain some associations with greater clarity if they represent a hierarchical relationship, as illustrated in figure 8.5. They can formalize other maps by representing categories around the main topic as illustrated in figure 8.6.

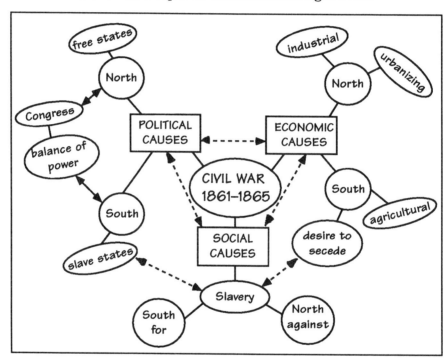

Figure 8.2. Mind map of Civil War. Reprinted from *Your Child's Growing Mind* by Jane Healy. Copyright © 1987 by Jane Healy. Used by permission of Doubleday, a division of Bantam Doubleday Dell Publishing Group, Inc.

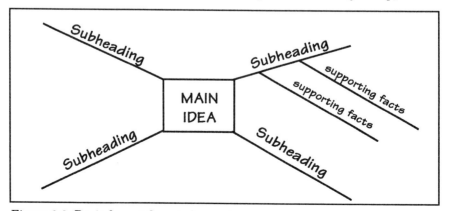

Figure 8.3. Basic format for mind mapping

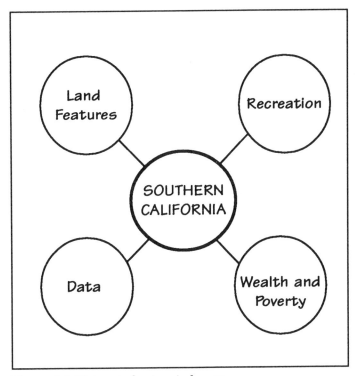

Figure 8.4. Using circles in mind maps

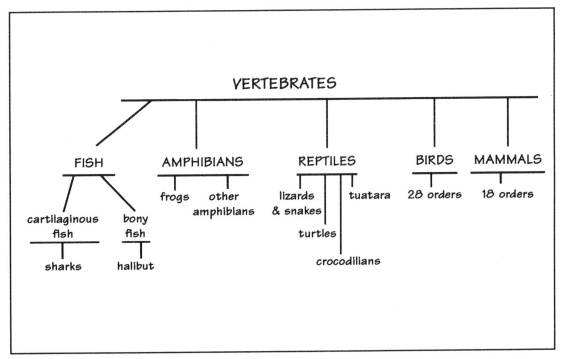

Figure 8.5. Hierarchical mind map

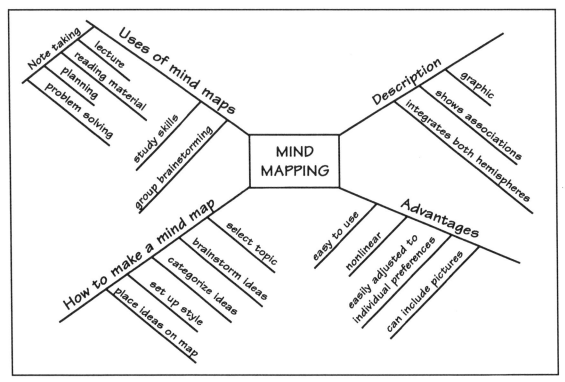

Figure 8.6. Formalized mind map

Basic Suggestions for Mind Mapping

- Use unlined paper.
- Print or write neatly.
- Use color to differentiate categories.
- Use connecting lines.
- Use any images and symbols you desire.
- Use arrows, codes, and symbols to show connections and associations among different groups.
- Draw boxes or rings around groups of concepts and images to create units.

Overview of Steps for Mind Mapping

1. Select a topic.
2. Brainstorm ideas.
3. Categorize and group ideas.
4. Set up style you will use.
5. Put main idea in center.
6. Add categories.
7. Add subcategories.

Mind Mapping to Aid Reading Comprehension

As a study tool, students, especially older students, can use mind mapping before and while reading a chapter. The mind map is an open-ended structure that helps students connect thought patterns rapidly and gives the students immediate feedback. It also helps students organize information visually before they read the chapter, which improves their comprehension and recall.

Before they read the chapter, students will place the main idea in the center of a page and each subheading (usually printed as a dark section subtitle) on a line coming out of the main idea to preview the story. As they read each section, they will write key words for the main idea under the appropriate subheading. This pattern allows students to insert information where they feel it is appropriate.

Pehrsson and Denner use the term *organizer* to refer to mind maps and suggest a variety of formats, two of which are the Episodic Organizer (figure 8.7) and the Cause/Effect Organizer (figure 8.8).[3]

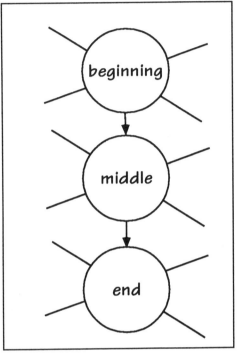

Figure 8.7. Episodic organizer. Reprinted from *Semantic Organizers: A Study Strategy for Special Needs Learners* by Robert S. Pehrsson and Peter R. Denner, pp. 75–76, with permission of Aspen Publishers, Inc., © 1989.

Figure 8.8. Cause and effect organizer. Reprinted from *Semantic Organizers: A Study Strategy for Special Needs Learners* by Robert S. Pehrsson and Peter R. Denner, pp. 75–76, with permission of Aspen Publishers, Inc., © 1989.

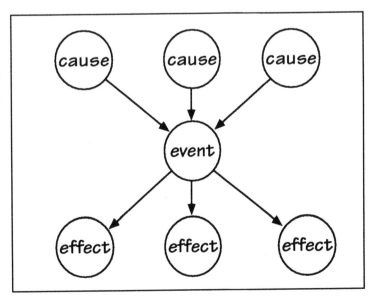

Using Mind Mapping to Help Beginning Writers

You can use mind maps to introduce young students to the concept that a paragraph is generally about a single topic. In simple writing, this single topic is represented by a word that tells who, where, or what. Depending on the age of the students, you may want to introduce the term *noun* at this point. Model the mind map by placing a word such as *elephant* on the board and drawing a box around it. Then ask students to suggest things that an elephant does or does not do, creating a mind map that resembles the one in figure 8.9. Following is a simple paragraph that might be derived from the mind map on elephants:

Elephants walk. Elephants eat a lot. Elephants swim. They do not jump.

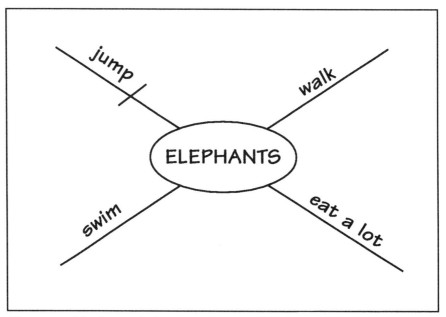

Figure 8.9. Mind map of what elephants do and don't do

As students become more proficient with the idea of nouns and related actions, they should expand to phrases. Figure 8.10 is an example of a mind map and the paragraph that a student wrote based on the mind map. Notice that characteristics that do not apply to hamsters are also included and are represented by a slash.

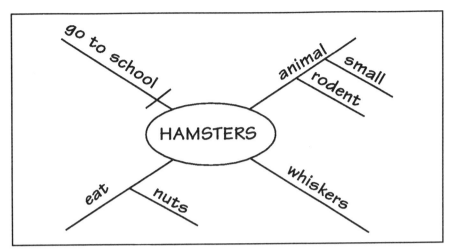

Figure 8.10. Mind map of hamsters

Hamsters are small animals. They are rodents.
Hamsters have whiskers. They like to eat nuts.
Hamsters don't go to school.

As students progress in their skills, you can reverse the process. Give them a simple paragraph and ask them to create a mind map based on the paragraph. This procedure will enable them to use mind mapping later to take notes while reading.

To expand this type of activity further, you can teach students to compare or contrast two animals or objects, for example, frogs and toads. First have students create a mind map for and write a paragraph about each animal. Then show the students how to reorganize the mind map, extending it for the task of comparing and contrasting (see figure 8.11).

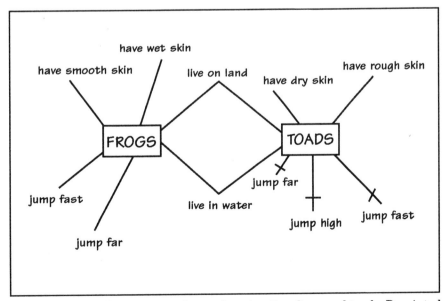

Figure 8.11. Mind map comparing and contrasting frogs and toads. Reprinted from *The Semantic Organizer Approach to Writing and Reading Instruction* by Robert S. Pehrsson and H. Alan Robinson, p. 84, with permission of Aspen Publishers, Inc., © 1985.

Mind Mapping to Aid Writing

Older students can use the strategy just described to write a report. They can organize the report first by using a mind map. They can then write the report one section at a time. Figure 8.12 shows an initial mind map that a young student used before writing the paragraph that follows it:

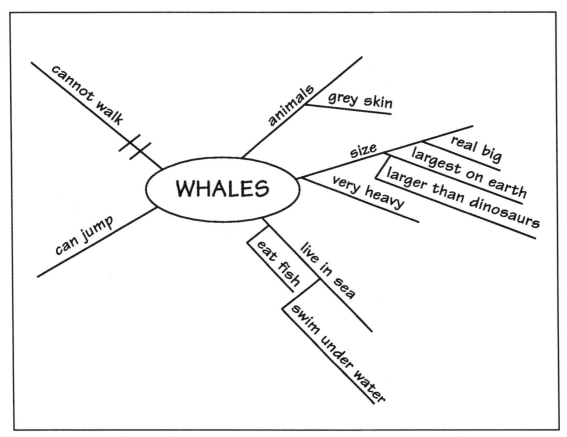

Figure 8.12. Mind map for paper on whales

Whales are the largest animals on earth. Whales are really, really big. Whales are larger than dinosaurs. Whales are very heavy. Whales live in the sea. Whales eat fish. Whales have grey skin. Whales can swim under water. Whales can jump. Whales can not walk.

A student's initial brainstorming session will often result in a poorly organized mind map. In these situations you will need to help the student learn how to organize a variety of random ideas into categories.

Mind maps can also help students organize larger research reports. To use mind maps for larger reports, however, the student should follow these seven consecutive steps:

1. Decide on the topic, being as specific as possible.
2. Brainstorm ideas important to the topic. Make a list or a mind map of as many topics as you can think of that relate to the overall main idea.[†]
3. Go systematically through the list you brainstormed. Eliminate ideas that do not seem relevant, and group the remaining items into groups that are cognitively similar. Each group will probably become a section within the main report.
4. Make a mind map for each section in the report. The mind map will be very simple at first, but you will add more areas as your research progresses.
5. Take notes on index cards while you research the topic. Number the notes and place corresponding numbers on the mind map so that you will have a reference number that helps you find the appropriate card when you are writing the details. You may enjoy using a different colored note card for each one of the sections.
6. Write the report one section at a time, organizing it using the PLEASE strategy (described in chapter 6).
7. Proofread each section of the report using the COPS strategy (described in chapter 6).

When students are brainstorming ideas for a research report, allow several days for step 2. Encourage students to think about the project and to make notes whenever ideas arise. During the "formal" brainstorming sessions, students can write these notes in their lists.

[†] For students to do their best writing, their right brains need to be allowed to contribute to the work. At times the right brain is on "automatic" and creativity is at its highest peak. These times may occur when students are showering, jogging, riding a bicycle, driving a familiar route, or just before they fall asleep. Tell your students to write down any creative ideas that the right brain produces as soon as possible; otherwise the ideas tend to be lost.

Children often become more creative while moving. Many children have excellent brainstorming sessions while wiggling over a large area.

Summary of Uses for Mind Mapping

- Note taking

    from a lecture
    from a text
    assignments that require gathering of information
    problem-solving tasks
    preparing a paper
    preparing a research report
    organizing ideas before answering an essay question
      on a test

- Study skills

    preparing for a test
    organizing for an oral report
    vocabulary words and meanings
    planning steps for a major project
    categorizing information

- Class preparation for a project. (These mind maps work well as a group effort, using a large flip chart or the chalkboard.)

    collecting data on a subject
    brainstorming ideas for a report
    clarifying concepts presented in a unit

9

Music and Rhythm
in the Classroom

You can use music, rhythm, and movement to create a relaxed, stress-free learning atmosphere. Such approaches help enhance integration and create a link between the right-brain's processing of music and rhythm and the left-brain's processing of verbal information. Rhythm has been found to generate automaticity of skills. Rhythm also has a socializing effect that frees a child from self-consciousness. It particularly benefits the child who finds it difficult to become part of the group.

Occupational therapists explain the benefits of music and rhythm by describing neurological integration and the coordination of different neuropathways. Perceptual-motor theorists indicate that the visual and auditory perceptions that the child must have in order to read and write are based on kinesthetic and tactile integration. For our purposes, it is sufficient to realize that the use of rhythm enhances automaticity while providing an activity that is a great deal of fun for children.

Suggestions for Using Rhythm in Reading Activities

General classroom music activities that include singing and rhythm help enhance the development of auditory discrimination skills, including integration of letter sounds, syllabification, and pronunciation of words. Choral reading is another rhythm activity that helps children develop fluency and rhythm in reading. Choral reading also provides children with a degree of "safety" that helps them gain confidence in their skills. Chanting is a related activity, but rather than reading with typical fluency, the children chant material in unison. Teachers most often choose poems and rhymes for children to chant.

Suggestions for Using Rhythm with Spelling

The following examples are some of the many creative lessons that you can initiate using rhythm and voicing. I recommend that you develop other activities to fit the age and interest level of your class.

Letter Chanting

Choral chanting is extremely helpful with spelling. It provides a way to incorporate rhythm and movement with a sequential task. The children say their spelling words and then chant each letter of the word. For variation they can chant in syllable patterns, with a pause between each syllable, which helps reinforce the concept of syllabification, an important aspect of both correct spelling and accurate reading.

Volume Changes

You can have students whisper vowels and shout consonants. Write a list of words on the chalkboard in large letters so the children have visual input while they are chanting the word. A list of five words is usually sufficient, but you can add more for older students. The class chants in unison, shouting when they say the consonants and whispering when they say the vowels, as in the following example (capital letters indicate letters to be shouted): T o R P e D o. You might also try having students shout vowels and whisper consonants: c O m p O n E n t.

These activities emphasize vowels. Vowels are often the tricky parts of spelling words, and by constantly reviewing and emphasizing the vowel sounds using rhythm, children will be better able to pay attention to such details.

Silent Alternation

Another activity that uses rhythm in chanting spelling words is alternating silent spelling with oral spelling. This activity works well with a metronome, but a metronome is not essential. You can either write the words on the board or select the five to ten hardest words from the week's spelling list. The number of words you write will depend on the age of your students. Point to the first word and ask the class to mouth each letter silently, keeping time with the metronome. It will help if you point to each letter on the beat of the metronome. The students spell the second word, shouting each letter, again in time to the metronome. They spell the third word silently and the fourth word out loud, alternating throughout the list. The class repeats the list, shouting the first word and alternating through the list so that the words that were silent the first time are shouted the second time.

Alternating Letters

Another rhythmic activity that helps children learn spelling words is to have the children take turns saying the letters. This activity helps children focus on the sequence of letters and helps develop automaticity.

Write the spelling list on the board. Divide the class into three to five groups, depending on its size. Group 1 stands up and says the first letter and then sits down. Group 2 stands up and says the next letter and sits down. Group 3 stands and says the third letter and sits down, and so on until you have cycled through all the groups. When each group has had a turn, begin again with Group 1. Each group should say its letter as the group stands up. You can synchronize the tempo with a metronome if you wish.

Suggestions for Using Rhythm with Math

Early elementary children have great fun marching and singing. You can encourage them to march around a large number written on the floor or chalked on the sidewalk or to play games such as "jump two times on the number 2." You can also hold up a card with a number on it and choose a student to tap a tambourine that number of times. You can establish a rhythm section using the number cues. You can also create other games using concepts of size (big, small), direction (near, far), or color.

Suggestions for Using Rhythm
in Teaching Multiplication Tables

You can use one of the many programs that have set the multiplication tables to music, such as Hap Palmer's *Singing Multiplication* or Ruth and David White's *Musical Math: Multiplication.*[1] A workbook that the teacher can use with the songs accompanies the latter program, which includes games such as "The Swing," "Basketball," and "Waterfall." Such games actively involve the students while they sing the facts, which greatly enhances the learning process.

Creative teachers can also set the multiplication tables to their own music and rhythm by chanting with or without a metronome or using a rap beat. You can also chant the poems in MFM, which helps develop automaticity by using alternative pathways to bring together and integrate information.

Combining a Balance Beam
or Trampa with an Academic Task

Some students, even at the college level, have said that they feel they can memorize better if they are moving. You can use a low balance beam (an 8-foot length of a 2-inch-by-4-inch board that is 2 to 4 inches off the ground) or a trampa (a 36-inch mini-trampoline or rebounder) with almost any academic task. The integration of these activities with thinking tasks encourages rhythm and movement and makes rote repetition tasks much more enjoyable. Following are sample activities that you can use to develop creative activities of your own.

Math Facts

Write a series of math facts on a large tagboard or the chalkboard. Students recite the facts as they walk or jump on the equipment. You can erase the answers as the students progress, encouraging students to visualize the missing number.

Spelling and Syllabification

Write a list of spelling words on the tagboard or chalkboard. Students read through the list saying one syllable per step or jump. As students progress, they should first say the syllables of each word and then spell the word, saying one letter per step or jump.

Spelling and Visualization

This activity is also called *RSV* because the steps are **r**ead, **s**pell, **v**isualize. Write a list of spelling words on the tagboard or chalkboard. Students read through the list saying one syllable per step or jump. As students progress, they should say the syllables of each word and immediately spell it, saying one letter per step or jump. The next step (visualize) requires students to "turn around and see the word(s) in their minds' eyes." They imagine reading the letters of each word. To help students take responsibility for their own learning, encourage them to decide how many times they want to repeat "read" and "spell" before progressing to the "visualize" step.

You can create similar activities for facts to be memorized, sentences, reading charts (such as a chart of random *b, p, d,* and *q* letters), or sequences of pictures. When jumping on the trampa, students should jump once without saying anything for each space in a sentence.

Be Creative

You will need to be creative and use your imagination to develop activities that use music and rhythm to enhance students' success, but you will also have fun. Your students will have more fun, be more motivated, and generally remember more efficiently. Your students who prefer right-brain processing will thrive on such activities.

10

Visual Strategies in the Classroom

V isual strategies are useful techniques that help emphasize right-brain processing skills that involve space, orientation, color, and holistic relationships. Visual strategies differ from imagery in that imagery requires the learner to provide the visual cues internally. Visual strategies overtly place the visual cues within the information. You may incorporate visual strategies directly into the concept, word, or unit you are teaching to increase learning efficiency. I have suggested the following ideas and guidelines to inspire other ideas.

Visual Strategies for Spelling

Weekly Spelling Lists

Select the three or four trickiest spelling words each week and develop a visual strategy for each one. The key to a good strategy is to determine what part of the word will be hardest for your students to remember, then to develop a way to emphasize that part of the word using size or exaggeration. Color exaggerates the part of the word very well and enhances learning. For example, *ie* is the trickiest part of the word *friend,* so you would write the word as follows: frIEnd. In the word *separate* the middle *a* is an unaccented syllable and students may have difficulty remembering that part of the word. When you write the word, you can write the *a* larger than the rest of the letters: sepArate. You can also exaggerate the pronunciation by saying "sep-ae-rate."

Written Work

Select those words that students frequently use but misspell. Use the same types of emphasis discussed earlier, but display the tricky words as the students write. After the students become more comfortable with a word, erase that word and add new words that present problems.

Configuration Clues

Help students become more aware of the visual configuration of words by playing configuration games. Write a list of words on cardboard or tagboard, being sure to choose words that have different configurations, and ask students to draw the outline of the words (see figure 10.1). Then have them cut out the words along the outline. They cover up the letters and try to guess the word based on its configuration (figure 10.2).

Figure 10.1. Word configuration of "school"

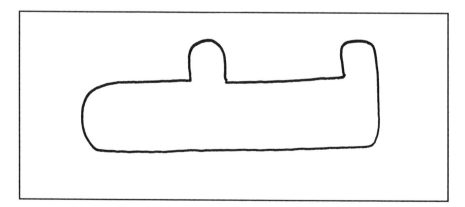

Figure 10.2. Word configuration of "school" with letters covered

To play a memory game using the configurations students have created, have students trace the configurations on plain tagboard and cut out the shapes. Then give them another list of the same words and have them write each word on a rectangle that is about the same size as the cut-out shapes. Working in pairs, they spread the shape cards and the rectangles upside down and play *memory*. They try to match the configuration card with the correct rectangular card. The first student's turn continues as long as she or he makes correct matches. When she or he misses, the next student takes a turn. If there is any doubt about the match, the students can compare the blank configuration to the original configuration card that has the word written within the shape. This game offers an additional challenge because students must visualize the configuration when it is turned upside down. When they turn over the selected shape, they see the configuration as it directly matches the word. If students need to make the game easier, they can play with the cards face up.

Visual Strategies in Decoding

Decoding is an important aspect of learning to read. Many students do not understand the prerequisite concept that each sound in a word can be represented by one or more letters. Blending practice helps solidify this important concept. If you combine blending with a visual tracking strategy, you enhance the positive effects of the activity.

Reviewing a Single Vowel Sound

The students will use choral reading for this activity. Prepare a chart like the one that follows if you are working with an individual student or if you are a home schooler. Omit the row of numbers in your chart; I include them here only for ease of reference. If you are working with groups, you should make five to ten rows but only five columns. I have included sample full-page charts in Appendix C. Select consonant sounds that are familiar to the students. Select a single vowel sound, such as short /a/.

1	2	3	4	5
m	n	p	a	t
c	h	t	a	m
l	s	d	a	d

Tell students that they will be reading words that contain three sounds. They will read from each line three times. They read the sound for *m* (column 1), then move to the short vowel sound *a* (column 4), and the final consonant *t* (column 5): "m-a-t." Then they say the word: "mat." Next, they read the consonant sound in column 2 and blend it with the vowel and the final consonant: "n-a-t: nat." The third time, they say. "p-a-t: pat." They read the second line as follows:

c-a-m: cam

h-a-m: ham

t-a-m: tam

Students would continue reading until they had read through all the lines in this manner.

You can also make the chart so that the final sound varies:

m	a	d	m	t	(mad, mam, mat)
b	a	t	g	n	(bat, bag, ban)
r	a	n	t	g	(ran, rat, rag)

Reviewing and Reinforcing a Variety of Vowel Sounds

For this exercise, you create more complex charts than those you create for the previous activity. Again, set up the charts so that the variable sound is sometimes in the initial position and sometimes in the final position.

Variable Sound in Initial Position

l	c	n	a	p	(lap, cap, nap)
b	l	f	o	g	(bog, log, fog)
n	r	b	u	t	(nut, rut, but)

Variable Sound in Final Position

d	i	n	p	g	(din, dip, dig)
l	e	d	g	n	(led, leg, len)
t	a	p	b	n	(tap, tab, tan)

Visual Strategies in Creative Lessons

Endless possibilities exist for using visual strategies in creative lessons. You can have students make maps for a history lesson or create a time line for a period in history. If you are studying pioneer life, students may work in groups to write an imaginary journal that describes their adventures and difficulties along a wagon trail or in a small rural area. Older students may like to create a series of editorial cartoons about historical events and people such as Christopher Columbus. Younger students may like to draw a picture of an imaginary pet dinosaur and then write a story entitled "Adventures with My Pet Dinosaur."

Creative Uses to Supplement a Book Report

Students can incorporate visual strategies into a book report in many ways. Following are some suggestions that students may use in addition to or instead of a written report.

- Make a map showing where the story takes place.
- Make a story map of the book's main events.
- Create a scroll or hand-rolled movie to illustrate the story.
- Make a poster about the story.
- Make a model of some object that is important in the story. The object could be a house, a log cabin, a rocket, a vehicle, or even a mountain.
- Draw objects from the story, cut them out, and make them into a mobile.
- Draw a significant scene on construction paper cut to fit a coat hanger. Attach it to the hanger. Write a description of the scene and its relevance in the total story.
- Choose an idea or scene from the book and use old magazine pictures to create a collage.
- Make puppets of the characters and create a dialogue.
- Create a mural about the story. Use charcoal, crayons, cut paper, water colors, or another art form.
- Make a time line of the events in the story.
- Play one of the characters.
- Draw a cartoon strip based on one of the characters.

Visual Strategies to Teach Grammar

Grammar concepts are often very difficult for some students to grasp. It helps if you make this normally nonconcrete area as concrete as possible through the use of visual strategies, especially with the basic concepts. Visual cues will increase students' recall of grammar concepts because the concepts will mean more to the students.

Nouns

You can teach students initially that a noun is a "person, place, or thing." You can represent this concept fairly easily using simple drawings or pictures cut from magazines. Label and categorize each picture as a person, place, or thing. Introduce a variety of nouns in this way.

To reinforce the concept throughout the curriculum, select sentences from the students' reading material and ask questions such as the following:

"What word tells us *who* is there?"

"What word tells us *where* they are?"

"What word tells us the *thing* that is red?"

You may ask similar questions about words in a spelling list. Examples include "Find a word that names a place" or "Find a word that is a thing or an object."

Prepositions

You can teach prepositions easily using visual strategies. Make a model of an airplane from paper or use a small plastic plane. Make a large paper cloud. Use the plane to demonstrate prepositional phrases: The airplane is *in* the cloud, *around* the cloud, *through* the cloud, *over* the cloud, and so on (see figure 10.3). Explain that the preposition is the word that describes the relationship between the plane and the cloud.

Visual Strategies in Foreign Language

Visual strategies can help make some aspects of teaching a foreign language more concrete. I use examples for teaching Spanish. Teachers of other languages can use these examples to stimulate visual strategies for their specific languages.

Students with a preference for visual strategies often respond well to verb conjugations that are *always* presented in the same visual format. The two-column model is easiest to use, with the singular conjugation on the left and the plural on the right.

Figure 10.3. Airplane going *through* cloud

You can adapt this model easily to explain the Spanish stem-changing verbs since these change their stems only in the singular forms and third person plural.

To teach basic conjugation, present the pronouns in the following order. Make sure that the students understand the meaning and usage of each pronoun by creating the chart in English first.

I	we
you (singular, familiar)	you (plural, familiar)
he, she, it, you	they, you (plural, formal)

You can then teach students the Spanish equivalents. Have students act out the words and demonstrate them with pictures to ensure that your students understand them. Then write each word on a separate word card and have students match it to its English equivalent. When students can match the words automatically, have them arrange the chart in Spanish.

yo	nosotros, nosotras
tú	vosotros, vosotras
él, ella, usted	ellos, ellas, ustedes

Some students will learn this pattern quite easily. Others will need to repeat it more often before they can match the words automatically. Students should understand the pattern fully *before* they begin to work with verb conjugations.

Teach students the endings for present tense -*ar* verbs, using any one of the traditional techniques. To review the endings and help students remember them automatically, have students create the pronouns chart. Write the present-tense -*ar* verb endings on different-colored index cards. Small cards, such as 3" x 2.5", work well. The students then match the verb endings to the appropriate pronoun, as illustrated in the chart below:

yo	-o	nosotros	-amos
		nosotras	-amos
tu	-as	vosotros	-áis
		vosotras	-áis
el	-a	ellos	-an
ella	-a	ellas	-an
usted	-a	ustedes	-an

Students should practice this matching task daily until it is extremely automatic. When they can automatically conjugate the -*ar* verbs, add cards for the -*er* endings. Use the same colors that you used for the -*ar* verbs unless the student is struggling to differentiate between -*ar* and -*er* endings.

Some students need to practice determining which pronoun to use in various situations and you could create charts that help them practice this skill. For example, you would write "Carlos y Juan" and they would choose the pronoun *ellos* (they). If you give them "Maria y yo," they choose the pronoun *nosotras* or *nosotros* (we).

Students who are learning a new language have traditionally used vocabulary flash cards. You can modify this technique into a visual matching activity to aid those students who prefer more visual processing. Write the English word on one card and the Spanish word on a different card, using a different color. Number the cards or code them in some other way so you can verify that the student is responding correctly. I prefer numbering the English cards in an upper corner and the Spanish cards on the reverse side. Students can use the cards for several different activities:

Activity 1: Match the Spanish to the English

Students spread out the English cards on the table and attempt to place the Spanish counterpart on top. Confirm that each match is correct immediately.

Activity 2: Match the English to the Spanish

This activity is the same as activity 1, except the students spread out the Spanish cards and place the English cards on top.

Activity 3: Concentration Game

The students mix the cards and place them face down on the table. Each student selects one card with a number on the back and tries to guess its match, which will be a card without a number on the back. A student may continue taking turns as long as she or he is making correct matches. When she or he misses, the partner takes a turn.

Activity 4: Traditional Flash Cards

You can drill students or they can drill each other or themselves by using the cards in the traditional manner.

11

Imagery in the Classroom

Many times students in our classrooms become inundated by facts. But they are in a hurry to complete an assignment in order to get to the next activity in their often busy lives, and they may not stop and realize the vast amount of information and experiences they have stored in their memories. How do they store this information? Children store much as visual images. Forming visual images is much like seeing a picture in your "mind's eye." Sometimes we tell children to "look at the blackboard in your mind" to help turn on their imagery systems. Visual images can be very colorful. They can also be noisy and full of movement, or they can be quiet and still but also very vivid. Encouraging students to enhance this natural ability often benefits their learning and retrieval systems tremendously.

You can help children develop and enhance this visual imagery fairly easily by using the visual strategies discussed in chapter 10. But imagery goes even further and you can use it to introduce concepts and ideas in most academic areas.

Types of Visual Imagery

Students generally begin the process of planned imagery by picturing an image of a person, place, or event. The extent of each image will vary greatly from person to person, but you can enhance students' skills in this area by carefully questioning them as they develop the image. Many students learn to develop and enhance the imagery process by imagining themselves performing an activity such as riding a bike, swimming a lap, or eating ice cream.

Some images elicit an emotional response, such as happiness, sadness, or fear. A complete visual imagery will result in children finding meaning in and making a connection between events or ideas. Being in a relaxed state greatly helps the development of an image, and many people recommend combining relaxation exercises with the imagery process. Relaxation helps the image develop and also helps students concentrate fully so that they can maintain and enhance the image.

How Can You Enhance Visual Imagery?

In order for students to progress in their use of imagery, they must accept the visual, nonverbal aspect of imagery. Children often accept the visual more easily than adults because children have had less verbal conditioning. Avoid using judgmental language ("that's a good picture," "that's right," "that's wrong") because it can destroy an image a child is developing.

The ability to concentrate completely helps imagery develop. Some students repeat the same image several times. Each time they conjure up the image, they find that it has more or sharper details, colors, shapes, textures, or movement.

Beginning Imagery Activities

You may help students develop imagery by starting with very concrete common activities. Following is an example that uses a comb as the focus for the image. To begin the activity, hold up a comb and have students study it silently for about thirty seconds. Instruct them to relax and then close their eyes. Verbally guide them through the imagery. Speak slowly to allow time for them to develop the image.

> See the comb in your mind's eye.
>
> See its color.
>
> Feel the comb in your hands.
>
> See the points on the comb.
>
> In your mind's eye, run your fingers along the teeth.
>
> See the color. Feel the points.
>
> (Pause)
>
> When I count to three, open your eyes.

After the imagery, allow the students time to touch the comb and ask them if what they felt in their imagery was the same or different. Accept either response; the purpose of the activity is to learn how to manipulate the image in the mind's eye, not to find a certain answer.

After students have experienced imagining concrete objects, expand to imagining activities. Following is an example using a carrot as a focus. Again, speak slowly to allow students time to develop their images:

> Close your eyes and relax.
>
> In front of you on a bright green tablecloth is a large orange carrot.
>
> It is a fat carrot, but it gets skinnier at the bottom.
>
> See the colors.
>
> See the shape.
>
> See the texture in the carrot's skin.
>
> (Pause)
>
> Now imagine yourself picking up the carrot. You are holding the carrot. Feel the weight of the carrot in your hands.
>
> (Pause)
>
> Now bring the carrot to your mouth.
>
> Take a bite.
>
> Hear the crunchy sound.
>
> Enjoy the taste.
>
> Chew the carrot carefully.
>
> (Pause)
>
> Look at the carrot again.
>
> See its color.
>
> Feel its texture.
>
> Place it back on the bright green tablecloth.
>
> (Pause)
>
> Now, when I count to three, open your eyes.

You do not need to read these imagery scripts verbatim. I have included them to help you develop other creative imagery scripts. I encourage you to use a variety of objects and activities.

When students seem to have mastered imagining objects, progress to people or pets. You should encourage students to imagine someone close to them: their mother, grandfather, or their pet dog, for example. You can add feelings to the scripts easily when you are directing your students in an imagery involving people or pets:

- You feel happy to see your dog.
- You feel your dog's warm fur next to your skin.
- You can see the expression on your mother's face. She looks happy. You feel happy.

Using Imagery with Social Studies

You can use imagery in social studies to help students relate to a concept within a unit. Following are examples using the American colonial period. Notice how these examples incorporate fantasy in the visual imagery. Remember that these examples are only guides and you should adjust them to the topic you are emphasizing. Again, speak slowly, pausing to allow students to form vivid mental pictures.

Colony Exercise

> You are a colonist in one of the American colonies. You and your family have moved to this area, and along with a few other settlers, you've cleared land. See yourself. See the clothes you are wearing. (Pause) See the land. See yourself with the others. See yourself clearing the land. (Pause) Begin to build a small wood cabin. See yourself carrying the wood. The wood is heavy. (Pause) You realize that the weather's beginning to turn colder. Feel yourself shiver. See yourself rushing to finish your preparations for winter before the snows come.

You could use this exercise to introduce a writing activity. Ask your students to write about their imaginary new home and the coming winter, focusing on their feelings. You could also use the activity to introduce an art activity; have students draw the wood cabin they are building within the colony. As a variation, lead the students through an imagery in which they are the cabin (feeling cold, yet feeling important because the family depends on you) or in which they are a piece of land being cleared for the new colony (feeling sad at losing your trees, homes for the animals, but also excited about the new colony).

The Presidents

You can use the peg-word system introduced in chapter 2 to help students remember the presidents of the United States. Remember that the system serves only as a cue to help students remember something they already know, so they will need to be familiar with the presidents' names. The following sample illustrates how you might teach the associations for the first five presidents. You can use the peg words for six through nine to teach the next four presidents. To continue, you will need to develop new words that rhyme with the numbers above nine and teach the rhymes in the same way that you taught the first nine peg words.

> *Teacher:* Class, remember the peg words we learned before. Let's review. (Allow time for the class to respond using each peg word: 1 is sun; 2 is shoe; 3 is bee; 4 is door; 5 is hive; 6 is ticks; 7 is Kevin; 8 is gate; 9 is sign.)
>
> Now we are going to learn the presidents of the United States in order. We will use our peg words to help us remember the order.
>
> Okay, president 1 is Washington. What is our word for 1? Right, it's sun. Can you picture some *washing* hanging out in the *sun?* The wash is on a clothesline and it is hanging in the bright sun. See it. Feel the hot sun. Remember: one—sun—washing. Our first president is . . .
>
> *Class:* Washington.
>
> *Teacher:* President 2 is Adams. Our word for 2 is shoe. Imagine a shoe hitting you in the *Adam's apple.* Can you see it? Picture the shoe coming right toward your Adam's apple. See it. Touch your Adam's apple. Remember: two—shoe—Adam's apple. So we remember president 2 is . . .
>
> *Class:* Adams.
>
> (Review the two associations. Use cues such as "see it," "picture it," and "feel it" to encourage students to visualize the associations.)
>
> *Teacher:* President 3 is Jefferson. Our word for 3 is bee. Imagine *Jeff's son* is trying to protect himself from a bunch of bees that are flying toward him. Hear the bees. See *Jeff's son* wrapping himself in *fur.* Can you see Jeff's son wrapped in the fur? What does it remind us of? Jefferson. See it. See the bees going toward Jeff's son who is all wrapped in fur. Picture it. Remember: three—bee—Jeff's son in fur. So we remember president 3 is . . .

Class: Jefferson.

(Review the three associations. Encourage the students to visualize and picture the images. Then review the three presidents in random order as quickly as possible without leaving some students behind.)

Teacher: President 4 is Madison. Our word for 4 is door. See a man who is *mad at his son* so he is slamming the door. (Make a motion of slamming a door.) See the door slam. Hear the door slam. Why is he slamming the door?

Class: Because he is mad at his son!

Teacher: Right, 4 is Madison. Our word is door so we think of a man who is mad at his son so he slams the door. Picture it. See it. Hear it. Feel the vibration of the door slamming. Remember: four —door—mad at his son. So we remember president 4 is . . .

Class: Madison.

(Review the four associations. Review them in sequence, forward and backward, and then in random order.)

Teacher: President 5 is Monroe. Our word for 5 is hive. Do you remember the movie star, Marilyn Monroe? Picture Marilyn *Monroe* with a giant beehive hairdo (demonstrate a very large hairdo). Can you see it? Picture it. See Marilyn Monroe with that huge beehive hairdo. Remember: five— hive—Monroe with hive hairdo. So we remember president 5 is . . .

Class: Monroe.

Remember to review after you establish each new association. Following are suggestions for associations for the next four presidents. You or your students may develop others.

President J. Q. Adams

6 is ticks; picture a curly J and a curly Q wiggling with the ticks.

President Jackson

7 is Kevin; picture a boy with Kevin written on his shirt playing jacks.

President Van Buren

8 is gate; picture a van burning by a big gate.

President Harrison
> 9 is sign; picture a hairy son holding a sign, such
> as a picket sign.

Using Imagery with Science

It is fun to use imagery with science because science is such a visual subject and it lends itself so easily to manipulation. Following are examples of how to use imagery in science. Use these examples as guides to develop imagery for your curriculum area.

• After a lesson on cell shape and cell division, encourage the students to close their eyes and imagine that they are a particular kind of cell. Write a guided imagery (similar to the colony guided imagery above) that describes their cell design and their cell activity.

• After a unit on dinosaurs, create a guided imagery. Have students imagine they are going on a time journey to the Jurassic Era. Have them visualize dinosaurs and the environment in which the dinosaurs lived. Also, have them visualize what the dinosaurs may have eaten.

• While teaching a unit about plants, create a guided imagery about being a seed and feeling yourself grow to introduce and expand the unit. Begin with the students pretending that they are seeds. Have them feel their bodies within the soil. Encourage them to feel elements such as rain and sun. Guide them through sprouting, pushing up through the earth, stretching, and growing. Encourage them to smell the smells that a new seed just coming up from the ground might have. Encourage images of color, movement, and tactile sensations.

You can combine imagery with metaphors for dramatic learning effects. For example, you can ask students how they feel when they are cold. What do they do? Many say they curl up. Next, ask them what happens to a mercury thermometer when it is cold. Encourage a comparison by asking, "How is that like what you do when you are cold?" These types of questions encourage metaphoric thinking. Follow these questions with a guided imagery in which the students imagine being very cold and curling up, and then imagine they are the molecules of mercury in a thermometer. They bunch up when they are cold and expand when they are warm.

Use of Imagery with English Activities

You can use imagery to help students develop and expand their creative writing experiences. You can begin by showing younger students a group of objects. Have them brainstorm as many words as they can think of that describe the objects. Then encourage the students to write about their own interpretations of the objects. Encourage creative spelling (phonetic spelling that is logical) at this level so that students concentrate fully on communicating in writing. Save proofreading for later in the process.

You can also give students a detailed, colored picture from a magazine and encourage them to visualize as much as they can about anything related to that picture. You can use this exercise as a group brainstorming activity. Then you can encourage students to write about their own interpretations of the picture.

=====12=====

Positive Suggestions

The right hemisphere helps process emotional responses. Right-hemisphere processing causes people to want to feel appreciated and valued, so it is important that you offer steady, genuine positive reinforcement. Teaching your students to use positive suggestions in cuing their own behavior will prove valuable in helping each student develop a positive emotional framework in which to work.

Positive Self-Talk

Self-talk is the process of using inner language to talk with oneself. Students who talk through a problem mentally before charging into action do better in school and demonstrate better problem-solving and analytical skills. They also seem to develop a higher level of thinking skills, perhaps because self-talk gives them more practice with verbal thinking. To enhance this positive emotional framework, encourage students to use positive self-talk.

You can model positive self-talk for students and encourage them to adopt such behavior. If you make a mistake in front of the class or cannot answer a question, use the opportunity to model self-talk that exhibits good problem-solving skills. For example, suppose a student faced with a long division problem gets "stuck" and cannot remember what steps to perform. If you have modeled problem-solving self-talk, she may be able to work through the problem in the following manner:

> Let's see. I'm having trouble solving 219 divided by 3, but I know if I just relax, I really can do this. What was that trick I learned? Oh, yes: "Dear Miss Sally Brown." Let's see, "dear" starts

with "d" and reminds me to do division first. So I will try to divide 3 into 2. No good. So I'll try 3 into 21. That works. It's 7. I put the 7 here, above the 1.

$$\begin{array}{r} 7 \\ 3\overline{)219} \end{array}$$

Now what do I do? Let's see, "miss" starts with "m" and that means multiply. 7 x 3 is 21. I put the 21 underneath.

$$\begin{array}{r} 7 \\ 3\overline{)219} \\ 21 \end{array}$$

Now what? Okay, "Sally" starts with "s" for subtract. 21 - 21 is 0.

$$\begin{array}{r} 7 \\ 3\overline{)219} \\ \underline{21} \\ 0 \end{array}$$

Well, that was easy.
What's next? "Brown" starts with "b" for bring down. So, I bring down the 9 and start over again with divide. I can do this!

$$\begin{array}{r} 7 \\ 3\overline{)219} \\ \underline{21} \\ 09 \end{array}$$

Positive self-talk helps students develop positive attitudes. The combination of strategy and positive self-talk can create a very powerful package. Students may begin using a new strategy by giving themselves messages such as, "If I work hard while I use this strategy (mnemonic or other technique), I will remember the ideas more easily." It is important for students to understand the *purpose* of a strategy, and teachers need to model its successful use if it is to be successful.

Positive Cues

Encourage students to use positive suggestions or cues. Post the suggestions and cues around the room or write them on small cards and place them on different students' desks. Some examples follow:

- If you think you can, you can.
- I can (see figure 12.1).
- Good effort = good work.
- *Creating the Thoughtful Classroom* posters[1]

Relaxation

Relaxation is critical to learning. Experienced teachers know that students who are tense, stressed, or worried have a difficult time learning. The emotional center of the brain (the limbic system that underlies the cortex) is closely linked to the systems that "gate" the messages that pass into—or are kept out of—the thinking brain. In *Endangered Minds: Why Our Children Don't Think,* Jane Healy states,

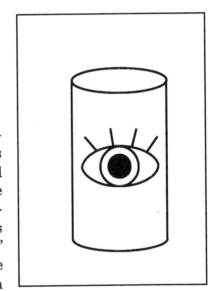

Figure 12.1. I can.

> If the emotional brain is preoccupied with fears or anxiety, it may fail to activate the proper cortical switches for attention, memory, motivation, and learning. High levels of stress can also change the fine chemical balance that enables messages to pass through all these systems; although the "good stress," generated by exciting and manageable challenges, may enhance learning, a child who is emotionally stressed may literally have trouble getting the brain's juices flowing for academics.[2]

You can help students relax by creating an atmosphere where they feel safe to take risks and experience learning. The use of positive suggestions greatly enhances students' ability to relax and learn more efficiently. To complement these strategies, you may also incorporate relaxation activities that use guided imagery.

Guided Imagery

The most common type of guided imagery activities for relaxation are those that have students sit comfortably with their eyes closed. You encourage students to concentrate on their breathing and use "easy breathing." You then lead them to visualize isolated limbs and areas of their bodies, one at a time, using visualization statements such as the following:

> Feel your legs; they feel heavy; they feel relaxed.
>
> Feel your feet; they are really heavy and relaxed.
>
> Feel your forehead; it is relaxed; it is smooth and loose.
>
> Use easy breathing; do not force it. Let your breath just flow . . . in . . . out . . . in . . . out.

Create a guided imagery that begins at the top of the body and moves down or one that begins at the toes and moves up. The result is the same: Students learn to relax individual muscle groups by concentrating on each group and imagining that it feels heavy and relaxed.

You can help some students relax by guiding them through imagery that helps them feel the contrast between tension and relaxation. Some teachers prefer to add this imagery to the easy breathing exercises in a darkened, quiet classroom. Following is an example of a guided imagery that uses contrast:

> Close your eyes. Sit comfortably. Make a fist in your right hand. Feel how tight it is. Now slowly, slowly open your fist. In your mind's eye see your fist opening. Feel it opening. It is feeling more relaxed. It is now feeling very relaxed.

You can have students tense any limb in the body and relax it in this manner.

To enhance the imagery, you may encourage students to imagine objects, such as the following:

> Imagine a butterfly on your open palm. See the colors on its wings. See it move its wings slowly. Feel the velvetlike texture of its wings.

> Imagine a marble on your open palm. (Continue developing the imagery by describing the marble's attributes.)

In *Using the Right/Left Brain: An Auditory Imagery Program,* Beverly Casebeer recommends using music in the background.[3] An excerpt from one of her relaxation exercises follows:

> Close your eyes. Think of a spot between your eyebrows. Concentrate on that spot as I talk to you. Listen to the soothing music, breathe calmly and quietly and deeply and relax. . . . Think about how relaxed your feet and legs feel . . .

Create Your Own

I have included this category to remind you that these activities are only guidelines. Use these suggestions to stimulate your own creativity in establishing a positive learning environment.

Teachers have been using positive suggestions of varying kinds in their classrooms since . . . who knows when? Good teachers automatically use such strategies because the strategies "work" or "feel right." Some teachers use the strategies deliberately to foster a positive and safe learning environment. Other teachers use many good techniques but are not aware that they do so; they teach more intuitively.

Whatever the situation in your classroom, work to become more conscious of how you structure the positive messages you give your students. Help your students to use positive suggestions so that they can internalize good feelings. Use the ideas suggested here to expand your techniques and strategies and to develop an even safer, more positive and enriching environment.

══════Conclusion══════

People ask, "What is this book about?" "Why would any teacher want to use alternative strategies?" "What kinds of benefits are there for students?" "What can a parent learn from a book such as this?" Here are some of the answers. You may think of many more; there is no limit.

• Alternative strategies help meet students' needs and begin where the student is.

• Alternative strategies create a safe place where students can take risks and try new learning skills.

• Alternative strategies create a learning environment where individual differences are respected.

• Alternative strategies provide a teacher with a large "bag of tricks" to use to meet individual needs.

• Alternative strategies help the student who learns differently.

• Alternative strategies generate creativity in students.

• Alternative strategies encourage higher levels of thinking, problem solving, and understanding.

• Alternative strategies are more fun for the students.

• Alternative strategies are more fun for the teacher.

• Alternative strategies offer a "ray of hope" to a child who might otherwise never be able to reach her or his full learning potential.

If this book helps one student love learning, it has been a success.

Appendix A
Peg-word Pictures
(chapters 2 and 3)

Following are the peg-word pictures for each number. You will need one copy of each when you are teaching the peg-word system in chapter 2. The pictures should be large enough for all students to see when you hold each picture up.

If you are going to use the pictures to teach the MFM system in chapter 3, you will need three copies of each.

══════ Appendix B ══════
Multiplication Rhymes
(chapter 3)

These rhymes were created by educational therapist Judy Love as a tool for learning multiplication facts. The rhymes and pictures are to be used in chapter 3.

$$3 \times 3 = 9$$

(bee bee sign)
Two bees flying in a line,
Ahead they see a honey sign.
Three times three equals nine. 9.

3 x 4 = 12

(bee door sun shoe)
The bee by the door has a good view;
He sees the sun wearing the shoe.
Three times four is a one and a two. 12.

$$3 \times 6 = 18$$

(bee ticks sun gate)

The bee and ticks will not be late.

They hurry to sit in the sun by the gate.

Three times six is a one and an eight. 18.

$$3 \times 7 = 21$$

(bee Kevin shoe sun)

The bee stung Kevin and that's no fun.

He's so mad he kicks his shoe at the sun.

Three times seven is a two and a one. 21.

$$3 \times 8 = 24$$

(bee gate shoe door)

The bee by the gate has a foot that's sore.

He got his new shoe stuck in the door.

Three times eight is a two and a four. 24.

$$3 \times 9 = 27$$

(bee sign shoe Kevin)

The bee on the sign looks up toward heaven.

He sees the shoe fall that was kicked by Kevin.

Three times nine is a two and a seven. 27.

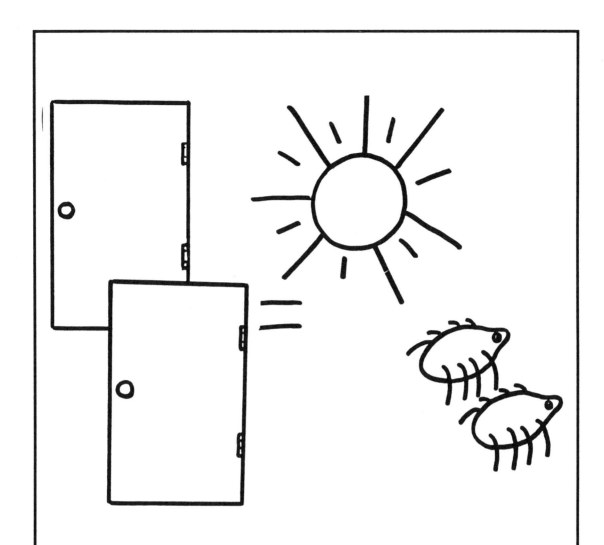

4 x 4 = 16

(door door sun ticks)
Past the doors both made of sticks,
We see sun shining on the ticks.
Four times four is a one and a six. 16.

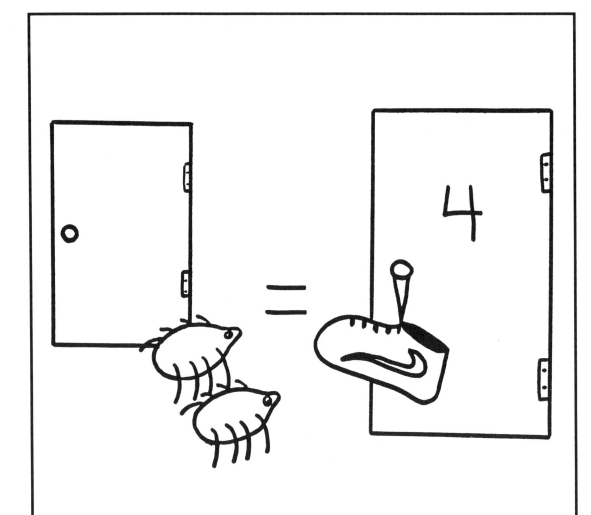

$$4 \times 6 = 24$$

(door ticks shoe door)
The ticks go past the little door
And hang a shoe on the door with the four.
Four times six is a two and a four. 24.

$$4 \times 7 = 28$$

(door Kevin shoe gate)

Out of the door runs Kevin, late;

He kicks his shoe right at the gate.

Four times seven is a two and an eight. 28.

$$4 \times 8 = 32$$

(door gate bee shoe)
Past one door and one gate, too,
We see the bee upon the shoe.
Four times eight is a three and a two. 32.

4 x 9 = 36

(door sign bee ticks)
The door and sign both have some nicks,
But not the little bee or ticks.
Four times nine is a three and a six. 36.

6 x 6 = 36

(ticks ticks bee ticks)
Ticks and ticks may nibble sticks,
But no sticks for this bee and ticks.
Six times six is a three and a six. 36.

$$6 \times 7 = 42$$

(ticks Kevin door shoe)
Ticks and Kevin feeling blue,
See the door beside the shoe.
Six times seven is a four and a two. 42.

$$6 \times 8 = 48$$

(ticks gate door gate)
Ticks on the gate just sit and wait;
They cannot open a door or gate.
Six times eight is a four and an eight. 48.

$$6 \times 9 = 54$$

(ticks sign hive door)
Ticks on a sign would surely roar
To see a hive knock on a door.
Six times nine is a five and a four. 54.

7 x 7 = 49

(Kevin Kevin door sign)
Kevin and Kevin hold a fishing line,
While past the door they see a sign.
Seven times seven is a four and a nine. 49.

7 x 8 = 56

(Kevin gate hive ticks)
Kevin stands by the gate doing tricks.
Watching him from the hive are the ticks.
Seven times eight is a five and a six. 56.

$$7 \times 9 = 63$$

(Kevin sign ticks bee)
Kevin goes past the sign to see
The little ticks beside the bee.
Seven times nine is a six and a three. 63.

$$8 \times 8 = 64$$

(gate gate ticks door)
Past one gate then one gate more,
See the ticks rest on the door.
Eight times eight is a six and a four. 64.

$$8 \times 9 = 72$$

(gate sign Kevin shoe)
The gate with the sign is bright and new,
And Kevin holds up his new shoe too.
Eight times nine is a seven and a two. 72.

$$9 \times 9 = 81$$

(sign sign gate sun)
Big sign and little sign both say fun.
It's fun to swing on a gate in the sun.
Nine times nine is an eight and a one. 81.

Chart 1: Reviewing a Single Vowel, Initial Sounds Change

m	n	p	a	t
c	h	t	a	m
l	s	d	a	d
s	g	l	a	s
g	t	n	a	b
b	f	r	a	n
s	l	w	a	g
p	r	j	a	m
n	g	r	a	p
b	f	c	a	t

Chart 2: Reviewing Multiple Vowels, Final Sounds Change

d	i	n	p	g
l	e	d	g	n
t	a	p	b	n
t	u	g	m	b
s	i	n	p	t
r	o	b	t	n
m	e	t	n	sh
r	a	m	p	t
d	i	p	m	sh
c	o	t	p	d

Chart 3: Reviewing Blends,
Final Sounds Change

c	l	a	p	d	n
b	l	o	ck	t	nd
c	r	a	b	ck	sh
f	l	a	t	sh	ck
b	r	i	ck	m	sk
p	r	o	d	m	p
t	r	a	p	mp	m
b	l	a	b	nd	st
d	r	u	m	g	nk
f	l	a	g	t	x

Key for Reading Chart 1

mat	nat	pat
cam	ham	tam
lad	sad	dad
sas	gas	las
gab	tab	nab
ban	fan	ran
sag	lag	wag
pam	ram	jam
nap	gap	rap
bat	fat	cat

Key for Reading Chart 2

din	dip	dig
led	leg	len
tap	tab	tan
tug	tum	tub
sin	sip	sit
rob	rot	ron
met	men	mesh
ram	rap	rat
dip	dim	dish
cot	cop	cod

Key for Reading Chart 3

clap	clad	clan
block	blot	blond
crab	crack	crash
flat	flash	flack
brick	brim	brisk
prod	prom	prop
trap	tramp	tram
blab	bland	blast
drum	drug	drunk
flag	flat	flax

Notes

Notes to Chapter 1

1. Robert Ornstein and Richard F. Thompson, *The Amazing Brain* (Boston: Houghton Mifflin, 1984), 21.

2. Jane Healy, *Endangered Minds: Why Our Children Don't Think.* (New York: Simon & Schuster, 1990), 66.

3. Ibid., 56.

4. Suzanne Stevens, *Classroom Success for the Learning Disabled* (Winston-Salem, N.C.: John F. Blair, 1984); Barbara Meister Vitale, *Unicorns Are Real: A Right-Brained Approach to Learning* (Rolling Hills Estates, Calif.: Jalmar Press, 1982); and Healy, *Your Child's Growing Mind: A Guide to Learning and Brain Development from Birth to Adolescence* (New York: Doubleday, 1987).

5. Clare Cherry, Douglass Godwin, and Jesse Staples, *Is the Left Brain Always Right?* (Belmont, Calif.: David S. Lake, 1989), 12.

6. Cherry, et al., *Is the Left Brain Always Right?* Vitale, *Unicorns Are Real;* Stevens, *Classroom Success for the Learning Disabled;* Suzanne Stevens, *The Learning Disabled Child: Ways that Parents Can Help* (Winston-Salem, N.C.: John F. Blair, 1980); Jane Healy, *Endangered Minds.*

7. Vitale, *Unicorns Are Real.*

8. Stevens, *Classroom Success for the Learning Disabled,* 284.

9. Ibid., 284.

10. Ibid., 23–24.

11. Healy, *Your Child's Growing Mind.*

Notes to Chapter 2

1. Regina G. Richards, *Visual Skills Appraisal: Appraisal of Visual Performance and Coordinated Classroom Activities* (Novato, Calif.: Academic Therapy, 1984); Regina G. Richards, *Classroom Visual Activities: A Manual to Enhance the Development of Visual Skills* (Novato, Calif.: Academic Therapy, 1988).

2. Ralph Garzia, OD, and Jack Richman, OD, *Developmental Eye Movement Test* (Version 1, 1987).

3. Albert Sutton, OD, *Vision, Intelligence and Creativity*. A series of articles from Optometric Extension Program Foundation (Foundation Curriculum, 1988–89), 8.

4. Homer Hendrickson, OD, *Spelling: A Visual Skill* (Santa Ana, Calif.: Optometric Extension Program Foundation, 1967). Pamphlet.

5. Ibid.

6. Harry Chapin, "Flowers Are Red," *Living Room Suite*. Electra Records, 1978.

7. Elliott B. Forrest, OD, *Visual Imagery: An Optometric Approach* (Duncan, Okla.: Optometric Extension Program Foundation, 1981), 32.

Notes to Chapter 3

1. J. E. Fleischner, et al., *Proficiency in Arithmetic Basic Fact Computation in Learning Disabled and Nondisabled Children* (Washington, D.C.: Office of Special Education, 1980).

2. Cuisenaire Blocks and Multi Links are trademarks of Cuisenaire Company of America, New Rochelle, New York.

Notes to Chapter 5

1. Anna Gillingham and Bessie Stillman, *Remedial Training for Children with Specific Language Disability in Reading, Spelling and Penmanship* (Cambridge: Educator's Publishing Service, 7th Edition, 1968; 20th Printing, 1991), 78.

2. Hendrickson, *Spelling*.

3. Gillingham and Stillman, *Remedial Training for Children*; Regina G. Richards and Jeralee Smith, *Memory Foundations for Reading* (Novato, Calif.: Academic Therapy, 1983); Beth H. Slingerland, *Basics in Scope and Sequence of a Multisensory Approach to Language Arts for Specific Language Disabled Children* (Cambridge: Educators Publishing Service, 1981).

Notes to Chapter 6

1. Francis A. Yates, *The Art of Memory* (London: Routledge and Kegan Paul, 1966).

2. Arthur Bornstein, "State and Capital Memorizer System," *Bornstein Memory Training Course* (Los Angeles, Calif.: Bornstein School of Memory Training, 1983).

3. Richards and Smith, *Memory Foundations for Reading.*

4. T. E. Raphaea, S. Englert, and B. W. Kirschner, "Students' Metacognitive Knowledge about Writing," *Research in the Teaching of English,* 23 (1989), 343–79.

5. Marshall Welch, "The PLEASE Strategy: A Metacognitive Learning Strategy for Improving the Paragraph Writing of Students with Mild Learning Disabilities," *Learning Disability Quarterly* 15: 119.

6. For a videocassette and instructor materials on the PLEASE strategy, write *P.L.E.A.S.E.: A Strategy for Efficient Learning and Functioning in Written Expression,* University of Utah, Department of Special Education, Educational Telecommunications, Salt Lake City, UT 84112.

Notes to Chapter 7

1. Bill Martin, Jr., *Sounds of Numbers,* teacher's ed. (New York: Holt, Rinehart, and Winston, 1972), TE74.

2. Ibid., TE77.

3. Linda Verlee Williams, *Teaching for the Two-Sided Mind: A Guide to Right-Brain / Left-Brain Education* (New York: Touchstone Books, Simon and Schuster, 1983), 62, 63.

Notes to Chapter 8

1. For a thorough discussion of mind mapping, its benefits and uses, and myriad examples, see Nancy Margulies, *Mapping Inner Space: Learning and Teaching Mind Mapping* (Tucson, Ariz: Zephyr Press, 1991).

2. Healy, *Your Child's Growing Mind,* 157.

3. Robert Pehrsson and Peter R. Denner, *Semantic Organizers: A Study Strategy for Special Needs Learners* (Rockville, Md.: Aspen Publishers, 1989), 75–76; Robert S. Pehrsson and H. Alan Robinson, *The Semantic Organizer Approach to Writing and Reading Instruction* (Rockville, Md.: Aspen Publishers, 1985), 84.

Notes to Chapter 9

1. Hap Palmer, *Singing Multiplication* (Freeport, N.Y.: Educational Activities, 1972); Ruth White and David White, *Musical Math: Multiplication* (Los Angeles: Rhythms Productions, 1978).

Notes to Chapter 12

1. Anne J. Udall, and Joan E. Daniels. *Creating the Thoughtful Classroom: Strategies to Promote Student Thinking* (Tucson, Ariz.: Zephyr Press, 1991). Book and posters are available.

2. Healy, *Endangered Minds,* 239.

3. Beverly Casebeer, *Using the Right/Left Brain: An Auditory Imagery Program* (Novato, Calif.: Academic Therapy, 1981, 71.

Bibliography

Bagley, Michael T., and Karin K. Hess. *200 Ways of Using Imagery in the Classroom.* Monroe, N.Y.: Trillium Press, 1987.

Bell, Nanci. *Visualizing and Verbalizing for Language Comprehension and Thinking.* Paso Robles, Calif.: Academy of Reading Publications, 1986.

Bornstein, Arthur. *Memory: Arthur Bornstein's Memory Training Course.* Dubuque, Iowa: Kendall/Hunt, 1979.

———. *Memory Power: Introduction to Memory Techniques.* Los Angeles: Bornstein School of Memory, 1986.

———. *Multiplication Memorizer.* Los Angeles: Bornstein School of Memory, 1982.

———. "State and Capital Memorizer System." *Bornstein Memory Training Course.* Los Angeles: The Bornstein School of Memory Training, 1983.

Bornstein, Scott. *Get Ready . . . Get Set . . . Read!* Canoga Park, Calif.: Memory Skills for Professional Advancement and Academic Achievement, 1991.

Campbell, Don G. *100 Ways to Improve Teaching Using Your Voice and Music: Pathways to Accelerate Learning.* Tucson, Ariz.: Zephyr Press, 1992.

———. *Sound Pathways: Using Your Voice and Music to Accelerate Learning.* Tucson, Ariz.: Zephyr Press, 1992. Audiotape.

Campbell, Don G., and Chris Boyd Brewer. *Rhythms of Learning: Creative Tools for Developing Lifelong Skills.* Tucson, Ariz.: Zephyr Press, 1991.

Canfield, Jack, and Harold C. Wells. *100 Ways to Enhance Self-Concept in the Classroom: A Handbook for Teachers and Parents.* Englewood Cliffs, N.J.: Prentice Hall, 1976.

Casebeer, Beverly. *Using the Right/Left Brain: An Auditory Imagery Program.* Novato, Calif.: Academic Therapy Publications, 1981.

Chapin, Harry. "Flowers Are Red." *Living Room Suite.* Electra Records, 1978.

Cherry, Clare, Douglass Godwin, and Jesse Staples. *Is the Left Brain Always Right?* Belmont, Calif.: David S. Lake, 1989.

de Bono, Edward. *Six Action Shoes.* New York: Harper Collins, Harper Business, 1991.

———. *Six Thinking Hats.* Boston: Little, Brown, 1985.

de Mille, Richard. *Put Your Mother on the Ceiling: Children's Imagination Games.* Santa Barbara, Calif.: Ross-Erikson, 1981.

Fleischner, J. E., N. D. Bryant, W. MacGinitie, J. Shepherd, and J. Williams. *Proficiency in Arithmetic Basic Fact Computation in Learning Disabled and Nondisabled Children.* Washington, D.C.: Office of Special Education, 1980.

Fogarty, Robin, James Bellanca, and Kay Opeka. *The Thinking Series.* Palatine, Ill.: Skylight Publishing, 1986–1990.

Forrest, Elliott B., OD. *Visual Imagery: An Optometric Approach.* Duncan, Okla.: Optometric Extension Program Foundation, 1981.

Galyean, Beverly-Colleene. *Mind Sight: Learning through Imaging.* Healdsburg, Calif.: Center for Integrative Learning, 1984.

Garzia, Ralph, OD, and Jack Richman, OD. *Developmental Eye Movement Test.* Version 1. South Bend, Ind.: Bernell, 1987.

Getman, G. N. *How to Develop Your Child's Intelligence.* Irvine, Calif.: Research Publications, 1984.

———. *Operational Vision.* Santa Ana, Calif.: Optometric Extension Program, 1960.

———. *Smart in Everything . . . Except School.* Santa Ana, Calif.: Vision Extension, 1992.

Gillingham, Anna, and Bessie Stillman. *Remedial Training for Children with Specific Language Disability in Reading, Spelling, and Penmanship.* 7th ed. Cambridge, Mass.: Educators Publishing Service, 1968.

Goode, Caron B., and Joy Lehni Watson. *The Mind Fitness™ Program for Esteem and Excellence: Guided Stories for Imagery in Whole-Brain Learning.* Tucson, Ariz.: Zephyr Press, 1992. Also available: *Reaching the Star Within.* Tucson, Ariz.: Zephyr Press, 1992. Audiotape to accompany *The Mind Fitness Program.*

Healy, Jane. *Endangered Minds: Why Our Children Don't Think.* New York: Simon and Schuster, 1990.

————. *Your Child's Growing Mind: A Guide to Learning and Brain Development from Birth to Adolescence.* New York: Doubleday, 1987.

Hendrickson, Homer, OD. *Spelling: A Visual Skill.* Santa Ana, Calif.: Optometric Extension Program Foundation, 1967. (pamphlet)

Hooper, Judith, and Dick Teresi. *The 3-Pound Universe.* Los Angeles, Calif.: Jeremy P. Tarcher, 1986.

Jensen, Eric. *Super-Teaching: Master Strategies for Building Student Success.* Del Mar, Calif.: Turning Point Press, 1988.

Klauser, Henriette Anne. *Writing on Both Sides of the Brain.* New York: Harper and Row, 1987.

Lazear, David. *Seven Ways of Knowing: Teaching for Multiple Intelligences.* Palatine, Ill.: Skylight Press, 1991.

————. *Seven Ways of Teaching: The Artistry of Teaching with Multiple Intelligences.* Palatine, Ill.: Skylight Press, 1992.

Levine, Mel. *Keeping A Head in School.* Cambridge, Mass.: Educators Publishing Service, 1990.

Link, D., and M. Welch. *Write, P.L.E.A.S.E.: A Strategy for Efficient Learning and Functioning in Written Expression.* Instructor's materials. Salt Lake City, Utah: University of Utah Educational Telecommunications, 1989.

Lyons, Emily Bradley. *How to Use Your Power of Visualization.* Red Bluff, Calif.: Lyons Visualization Series, 1980.

McCarthy, Bernice. *The 4MAT System: Teaching to Learning Styles with Right/Left Mode Techniques.* Barrington, Ill.: Excel, rev. 1987.

McKisson, Micki. *Chrysalis: Nurturing Creative and Independent Thought in Children.* Tucson, Ariz.: Zephyr Press, 1983.

Margulies, Nancy. *Mapping Inner Space: Learning and Teaching Mind Mapping.* Tucson, Ariz.: Zephyr Press, 1991.

Martin, Bill, Jr.. *Sounds of Numbers,* Teacher's Edition. New York: Holt, Rinehart, and Winston, 1972.

Mason, Kathy. *Going Beyond Words: The Art and Practice of Visual Thinking.* Tuscon, Ariz.: Zephyr Press, 1991.

Mastropieri, Margo A., and Thomas E. Scruggs. *Teaching Students Ways to Remember: Strategies for Learning Mnemonically.* Cambridge, Mass.: Brookline Books, 1991.

Morris, Susan, and Bernice McCarthy. *4MAT in Action II: Sample Lesson Plans for Use with the 4MAT System.* Barrington, Ill.: Excel, 1983.

Ornstein, Robert, and Richard F. Thompson. *The Amazing Brain.* Boston: Houghton Mifflin, 1984.

Palmer, Hap. *Singing Multiplication.* Freeport, N.Y.: Educational Activities, 1972.

Pehrsson, Robert S., and Peter R. Denner. *Semantic Organizers: A Study Strategy for Special Needs Learners.* Rockville, Md.: Aspen Publishers, 1989.

Pehrsson, Robert S., and Alan H. Robinson. *The Semantic Organizer Approach to Writing and Reading Instruction.* Rockville, Md.: Aspen Publishers, 1985.

Raphaea, T. E., S. Englert, and B. W. Kirschner. "Students' Metacognitive Knowledge about Writing," *Research in the Teaching of English* 23:343–79.

Richards, Regina G. *Classroom Visual Activities: A Manual to Enhance the Development of Visual Skills.* Novato, Calif.: Academic Therapy Publications, 1988.

———. *Visual Skills Appraisal: Appraisal of Visual Performance and Coordinated Classroom Activities.* Novato, Calif.: Academic Therapy Publications, 1984.

Richards, Regina G., and Jeralee Smith. *Memory Foundations for Reading.* Novato, Calif.: Academic Therapy Publications, 1983.

Rose, Laura. *Picture This: Teaching Reading through Visualization.* Tucson, Ariz.: Zephyr Press, 1989.

Rotalo, Susan. *Right-Brain Lesson Plans for a Left-Brain World: A Book of Lesson Plans for English and Speech.* Springfield, Ill: Charles C. Thomas, 1982.

Schnitker, Max. *The Teacher's Guide to the Brain and Learning.* San Rafael, Calif.: Academic Therapy Publications, 1972.

Slingerland, Beth H. *Basics in Scope and Sequence of a Multisensory Approach to Language Arts for Specific Language Disabled Children.* Cambridge, Mass.: Educator's Publishing Service, 1981.

Stevens, Suzanne. *Classroom Success for the Learning Disabled.* Winston-Salem, N.C.: John F. Blair, 1984.

———. *The Learning Disabled Child: Ways that Parents Can Help.* Winston-Salem, N.C.: John F. Blair, 1980.

Sutton, Albert, OD. *Vision, Intelligence and Creativity.* A Series of Articles from Optometric Extension Program Foundation Curriculum, 1988–89.

Tyler, Sydney. *Just Think* series (1–7). Montana, Calif.: Thomas Geale, 1982–1988.

Udall, Anne J., and Joan E. Daniels. *Creating the Thoughtful Classroom: Strategies to Promote Student Thinking.* Tucson, Ariz.: Zephyr Press, 1991. Book and posters are available.

Vail, Priscilla. *Smart Kids with School Problems: Things to Know and Ways to Help.* New York: Penguin, 1987.

Vitale, Barbara Meister. *Unicorns Are Real: A Right-Brained Approach to Learning.* Rolling Hills Estates, Calif.: Jalmar Press, 1982.

von Oech, Roger. *Creative Whack Pack.* Stamford, Conn.: U.S. Games System; New York: Harper Collins, Harper Perennial, 1992.

————. *A Kick in the Seat of the Pants.* New York: Harper Collins, Harper Perennial, 1986.

Wallace, Rosella R. *Rappin' and Rhymin' for Active Learning.* Tucson, Ariz.: Zephyr Press, 1992.

————. *SmartRope Jingles.* Tucson, Ariz.: Zephyr Press, 1993.

Webb, Terry Wyler, and Douglas Webb. *Accelerated Learning with Music.* Norcross, Ga.: Accelerated Learning Systems, 1990.

Welch, Marshall. "The PLEASE Strategy: A Metacognitive Learning Strategy for Improving the Paragraph Writing of Students with Mild Learning Disabilities," *Learning Disability Quarterly* 15:119.

Welch, M., and D. Link. *Write, P.L.E.A.S.E.: A Strategy For Efficient Learning and Functioning in Written Expression.* Video cassette. Salt Lake City, Utah: University of Utah Educational Telecommunications, 1989.

White, Ruth, and David White. *Musical Math: Multiplication.* Los Angeles, Calif.: Rhythms Productions, 1978.

Williams, Linda Verlee. *Teaching for the Two-Sided Mind: A Guide to Right-Brain/Left-Brain Education.* New York: Touchstone Books, Simon and Schuster, 1983.

Yates, Francis A. *The Art of Memory.* London: Routledge and Kegan Paul, 1966.

Additional Resources from Zephyr Press

MAPPING INNER SPACE
Learning and Teaching Mind Mapping
by Nancy Margulies

Mind mapping is a significant advance over traditional, linear note taking. Use mind mapping for personal note taking, in curriculum planning, in group process in the classroom, and as a teaching strategy in daily lessons.

Using a mind map, you can record more information on a page and show relationships among various concepts.

Mind mapping integrates the processes of both sides of the brain—the linear left side and the global right side.
ZB18W . . . $24.95

Students use the whole brain to memorize

RAPPIN' AND RHYMIN'
Raps, Songs, Cheers, and SmartRope Jingles for Active Learning
by Rosella R. Wallace, Ph.D.

This book and tape set uses the powers of rhythm and rhyme to teach children the information they need to know in a way they want to learn!

It's easy! Just play the lively cassette to teach your students the names of continents, oceans, and more. Side 1 features—The Fifty States, Planet Talk, Count by Sixes, and 12 additional songs and raps for math, geography, and more. Side 2 offers The Parts of Speech, Spelling Word Cheers, City-Comma-State Punctuation Rap, and 12 more beat-filled rhymes for learning vowels, suffixes, prefixes, contractions, and more.

With Rappin' and Rhymin' you can—

* Motivate student participation
* Engage students in large-group response activities
* Provide enrichment, experience joy, and relieve stress—all of which enhance learning
* Optimize learning—at home and in the classroom

Grades K-8.
ZB28W . . . $19.95

To order, write or call—

Zephyr Press
P.O. Box 66006-W
Tucson, Arizona 85728-6006
Phone—(602) 322-5090
FAX—(602) 323-9402

You can also request a free copy of our current catalog showing other learning materials that foster whole-brain learning, creative thinking, and self-awareness.

Listen to the heartbeat of your students

RHYTHMS OF LEARNING
Creative Tools for Developing Lifelong Skills
by Don G. Campbell and Chris Boyd Brewer

Here are more than 75 classroom activities to boost learning and provide opportunities for personal growth.

Learn about the physical and emotional highs and lows to promote a learning environment that is less stressful and more focused. Specific activities for teachers precede and complement the student activities.

You can—

* Discover the best learning modes of your students
* Learn to use music, art, movement, and drama to promote optimal learning states
* Use effective rhythms of presentation in your teaching
* Learn about and use the methods of Lozanov and Tomatis and the techniques of accelerated learning

Grades K-Adult.
ZB21W . . . $24.95

Children hop, skip, and jump— learning facts quickly and easily.

SMARTROPE JINGLES
Jump Rope Rhymes, Raps, and Chants for Active Learning
by Rosella Wallace, Ph.D.

Teach basic classroom facts fast with this fun, stress-free approach. With these rhymes and chants, you can teach your students more and increase their recall dramatically.

This one-of-a-kind collection can be used to teach—

* Multiplication tables
* State capitals
* Planets of our solar system
* Roman numerals
* And so much more!

Teachers and parents have used these chants and raps with children in the classroom, in special education programs, in ESL, on the playground, in P.E., and at home.

Grades 3-9.
ZB35W . . . $14.95

Zephyr Press

REACHING THEIR HIGHEST POTENTIAL